FROM CONFLICT TO CONNECTION

FROM CONFLICT TO CONNECTION

Nonviolent Communication for Saying What You Feel

(Not What You'll Regret)

MICAH SALABERRIOS

SHAMBHALA

Shambhala Publications, Inc.
2129 13th Street
Boulder, Colorado 80302
www.shambhala.com

Cover art: Liliya Rodnikova/Adobe Stock
Cover design: Daniel Urban-Brown
Interior design: Anna Becker

9 8 7 6 5 4 3 2 1

First Edition
Printed in the United States of America

Shambhala Publications makes every effort
to print on acid-free, recycled paper.
Shambhala Publications is distributed worldwide
by Penguin Random House, Inc., and its subsidiaries.

LIBRARY OF CONGRESS CATALOGING-IN-PUBLICATION DATA
Names: Salaberrios, Micah author
Title: From conflict to connection: nonviolent communication
for saying what you feel (not what you'll regret) / Micah Salaberrios.
Description: First edition. | Boulder, Colorado:
Shambhala Publications, Inc, [2026]
Identifiers: LCCN 2026005565 | ISBN 9781645473725 trade paperback
Subjects: LCSH: Conflict management |
Interpersonal communication | Nonviolence
Classification: LCC HM1126 .S25 2026
LC record available at https://lccn.loc.gov/2026005565

The authorized representative in the EU for product safety and compliance
is eucomply OÜ, Pärnu mnt 139b-14, 11317 Tallinn, Estonia,
hello@eucompliancepartner.com.

CONTENTS

FROM CONFLICT TO CONNECTION

INTRODUCTION

We were six months into working side by side, eight hours a day, on a feature-length documentary. I was the editor, and she was the writer-producer. We were both excited about the project and knew that the information in it had the potential to change the lives of thousands, if not millions, of people for the better.

The first few months had flown by. Everything flowed seamlessly without a single issue. We were in sync on nearly every decision, and every day at work was a pleasure. Unfortunately, after about three months of harmony, small irritations began to pop up for each of us. Nobody wanted to rock the boat, so we generally just brushed them aside and kept working.

By month four, several clear creative differences arose. Nothing unmanageable, but the cracks were starting to show. We were getting closer to some deadlines, so stress levels were on the rise.

Month five was when I realized our issues had become too significant to leave unaddressed any longer. Creative disagreements became a frequent occurrence, and our tones grew sharper. We made a couple attempts to talk, but they ended with nothing resolved. Though we remained civil on the surface, the friction was undeniable. I began to wonder if it was time for me to leave the project.

Finally, in month six, it all came to a head. Up to this point, we had more or less pushed any serious disagreements under the rug but, as the Canadian psychologist Jordan Peterson has coined,

"Conflict delayed is conflict multiplied"—and things were certainly ready to multiply.

I had been working from home for a few days on an assignment the producer had given me. As I got started, I realized that to complete it properly, I first needed to tackle some other tasks. These other tasks led me to find some previously unexamined footage that I immediately recognized would be a huge benefit for the film. I spent the entire weekend digging through the new footage, finding nugget after nugget of documentary gold. When I returned to the office, I was brimming with excitement to show the footage to her and the director, who had stopped by that day. To my surprise, she didn't share my enthusiasm in the slightest. Instead, she was upset that the specific task she'd assigned had not been completed. I tried to explain that in order to complete her assignment, I had to handle some overlooked tasks first, which led me to all this great new footage. Yet nothing I said was getting through. Frustration quickly built in both of us and our tones became undeniably harsh.

I knew that if she would just take a moment to look with an open mind at what I'd found, she'd be as excited as I was. The new footage solved several issues we had been grappling with for months in the film. Instead, she kept repeating that I should've done what she'd originally asked. She even accused me of being "irresponsible," questioning how she could trust me in the future. I would've been frustrated no matter the circumstance, but for this to happen in front of the director only amplified the tension. It was in that moment that all the passion I had left for the project seeped out of me. The urge to quit and walk out was overwhelming. All of the tensions we'd been bottling up over the past few months came flooding out, and I could barely contain my emotions.

In my opinion, she was treating me like an amateur, as if I didn't know what I was doing, despite having several distinguished credits under my belt. I didn't have to tolerate this level of disrespect. I had dedicated six months to this project and given it everything I had. If she wanted someone to follow orders like a mindless robot, she could find someone else!

I was two seconds away from leaving the project when she looked at me, softened her tone, and asked, "Are you upset because you would like more appreciation for all the passion and expertise you're bringing to this project?" Her question and the warmth in her tone caught me off guard, and I sat there in silence. That was *exactly* how I felt. How did she know? I had been bracing for another wave of criticism and condescension but instead received a question about how I was feeling and why. I had been so prepared for confrontation that when I instead received empathy, it bypassed my defenses and went straight to my heart.

Tears of relief welled up in my eyes. I genuinely cared about this project and didn't want to leave on such bad terms. Her question instantly let me know she understood where I was coming from, and I felt a calm settle over me. There was no longer anything for me to defend or declare. Suddenly it seemed like we were both on the same team again.

My whole body language changed as I said, "Yes. That's exactly how I feel!" We hugged and smiled, and in that moment, all the tension between us lifted. We talked for a few moments and then with this newfound feeling of connection, she decided to look at the new footage and agreed with me that it was great and would help solve several issues. I also realized and admitted that I should have given her a heads-up instead of surprising her in front of the director.

This was a breakthrough moment for us on the project, and the camaraderie between us stayed at a high level long after that day.

Later, after the director left, she revealed she had used something called *Emergency Empathy* on me. I had no idea what that was, but I knew it was powerful and I needed more of it in my life. She explained that she'd been taking a Nonviolent Communication

(NVC) course for the past few weeks and in our conversation she had applied what she learned. This was how I first came across NVC, and it has profoundly improved my quality of life ever since. After that encounter, I began to study NVC nonstop every day for months. I couldn't get enough. This way of communicating was so different from anything I had ever come across. I knew that if I could fully integrate it into my life, all my relationships would improve. There was such consistent logic behind all of the teachings; and the more I learned, the more I *wanted* to learn. It was all I could talk about (much to some of my friends' dismay), and everything began to be filtered through NVC-tinted glasses. I found myself breaking down and analyzing movie scenes, conversations between strangers, conversations between me and my family, and especially any disagreements I was involved in.

At the time, I had an hour-plus commute to work each way, five days a week. I took that time to listen nonstop to the audiobook of *Nonviolent Communication* by Marshall Rosenberg—the creator of Nonviolent Communication—while reading the paperback at night and scouring the internet for workshops on the weekends. I quickly discovered that most NVC workshops were a bit expensive for me. At the time, they cost between $750 and $1,500 for a weekend course. I found one that was more affordable, but I left feeling extremely disappointed. The workshop was filled with language I'd never use in a real conversation. Plus, they were going over the concepts so slowly that, at the end of the first day, I walked away with only one new insight. To be fair, it was a good one, but this experience was nothing like the consistent stream of profound insights I'd received from Rosenberg's books and talks.

Frustrated, I decided to stick with learning straight from the source. I read and reread his book countless times and studied all of his recorded workshops intently. Gradually I began to grasp the concepts on deeper and deeper levels while seeing varying degrees of success as I practiced them in my personal life. When my NVC attempts worked, I felt elated and empowered. It was exhilarating to find solutions and avoid arguments using these new techniques. My whole future seemed brighter. Arguing with loved ones was so intense and painful that I was overjoyed knowing NVC worked in the real world. When it didn't work, though, I felt embarrassed and frustrated. Sometimes it seemed like my attempts at NVC made things worse. Not a great feeling. People would say, "Why are you talking so weird?" Or they would just stare at me like they didn't understand anything I was saying. Yet I persisted.

Every time I failed, I would go back and analyze the conversation. Where did it go wrong? What did I miss? Does NVC really work as well as I thought it did? Inevitably I would find a clear mistake on my part. I had either forgotten a step, slipped in a judgment, or made some other basic error. I would then return to Rosenberg's teachings and focus on the underlying principles I had missed. Once I fully understood the concepts, I would replay the conversation and correct my mistakes. I did this again and again for months. My failures became less and less and my successes more frequent. Over time, I realized I had a knack for understanding these concepts. Ironically, I even found myself coaching the producer on her own NVC attempts in her personal life, despite the fact that she'd already taken several courses on it.

One of the main reasons why I was so hyperfocused on learning NVC is because I recognized I was still carrying a lot of unhelpful communication patterns from my childhood. It was obvious to me that if I didn't put in some serious effort to correct these, I would never change. I'd grown up in a verbally volatile household. My father passed away when I was two, and though I always knew my mom loved me, she struggled to control her emotions. When she became upset with me or my two sisters, her weapon of choice was words, including name-calling, guilt trips, threats, and yelling. I don't blame her; I know she did her best with the knowledge she had while raising three children on her own in a stressful world. Today we have a great relationship, thanks in no small part to NVC.

Before learning NVC, my speech was riddled with judgments. I often blamed others for how I felt. I made demands, issued threats, and freely criticized, just as I had seen in my childhood. My life was littered with an array of intense arguments, hurt feelings, and fractured relationships. I would often avoid bringing things up that were bothering me because, more times than not, it would erupt into another intense argument. Even minor things could get blown way out of proportion. I had no idea how to navigate conflict in an efficient way.

Yet after only a few months of studying and practicing NVC, I saw significant improvements in all of my relationships. I could finally discuss any issue that was bothering me without making things worse. I, in turn, was easier to approach when someone had an issue to discuss with me. This was something I never knew was possible.

When I went home for the holidays that year, I spent the majority of my time teaching NVC to my entire family, from my sister and her four children to my mom and my cousins. Even my sister's neighbor wanted to learn. I noticed that I found myself repeating the same nuances to the basic concepts that nearly everybody seemed to miss. For example: the difference between an actual feeling, such as *sadness*, and a judgment disguised as a feeling, such as *disrespected*; or why any sentence beginning with "I feel as if . . ." was always followed by a judgment and not a real feeling. More on these points will be explained in the following chapters. It struck me that some of these nuances were not sufficiently addressed in any of the literature I had been studying. I attribute this to the fact that there have been significant cultural and communicative shifts since the original book on NVC came out in the seventies. We now live in a much faster-paced world, with infinite information at our fingertips, and this is reflected in how we learn and speak.

I decided to write a short manual on NVC to avoid repeating myself so often. Once I started writing, I discovered that I had more to say than my initial points, and I kept going until I had completed my first book, *The Art of Nonviolent Communication.*

I knew that without regular use, this knowledge had the potential to fade from my memory and I would likely resort to my old habits of communication. I had already met many people who claimed to have learned NVC years ago but were clearly not practicing it anymore. In an effort to avoid this happening to me, I started a podcast and began teaching workshops to keep it current in my mind.

Over the years, I have received many emails filled with heartwarming feedback from people who tell me I have helped save their marriage, repaired a family relationship, or even inspired several psychologists to use NVC in their practice. In fact, one psychologist told me the other day that he gives my audiobook to every one of his patients.

I am beyond honored to know that, in my small way, I am contributing to helping the world be a more loving, conflict-free place. I decided to write this second book because in the process of helping people over the past decade and practicing NVC in my own life, I have gained many new insights that I believe can help all of those brave souls on their journey to becoming great communicators.

This book is for everyone who

- is tired of painful, pointless arguments with loved ones and is willing to put in a bit of work to develop new communication skills;
- wants to be able to bring up sensitive topics without fear of instigating a conflict;

- desires to learn how to set clear, firm boundaries without sounding aggressive and creating further tension; and
- wants to have the ability to rapidly de-escalate intense interactions and skillfully deal with triggered people.

By learning basic NVC skills, and more specifically the tool of Emergency Empathy, you'll be able to fearlessly speak with authenticity and specificity while removing judgments and vague language. You'll be able to navigate sensitive topics with grace, and if you choose, you'll even be able to help guide loved ones through their own conflicts. This can all be done while sounding natural and conversational, which is one of the core concepts I emphasize in my approach to teaching NVC.

Emergency Empathy is what you will use to rapidly build connection with someone while they are upset or triggered. Once they feel calm, because they know they have been heard and understood, the four steps of NVC will guide you toward finding win-win solutions that are both achievable and sustainable. The skills taught in this book are simple, practical, and profound. They will consistently work in a vast variety of situations, as long as you follow the core principles. You can apply some of the core tools immediately and make a noticeable difference. However, if you truly want to become proficient at NVC and Emergency Empathy, it will require a small but significant investment of time and practice.

Learning NVC isn't just about understanding its rules; you need to rewire how you speak and respond in emotionally triggering situations. Learning this isn't the easiest task, but it may be one of the most rewarding. I can't promise you'll never get into another argument, but I can promise that if you stick with these techniques, you will drastically reduce the frequency and intensity of future conflicts.

I am incredibly grateful for the knowledge I have gained on my NVC journey and for the ways it continues to transform my life and relationships. It's a great honor to share this profound information with you, and I hope it enhances your life as much as it has mine.

ONE

Violent and Nonviolent Language

WHEN MOST PEOPLE hear the term *Nonviolent Communication*, there can be a disconnect because we tend to associate violence primarily with physical actions. *Physical violence is an act intended to inflict pain on someone.* Universally we know this is considered harmful and socially unacceptable, except in cases of self-defense or for the protection of others. Violent language is similar, though less obvious and often more socially acceptable. In fact, it's so embedded in the way many of us communicate that it often goes unnoticed. It shows up everywhere: in conversations with friends and family, in classrooms, in movies, in books, and across social media. It's so widespread, so normalized, that many of us don't even realize it's there.

So what really *is* violent language? How do we identify it? Simply put, violent language is any communication designed to make someone feel bad or that implies someone is wrong or bad. This can be done in a wide variety of ways, including, but not limited to, judgments, insults, ridicule, threats, demands, blaming, and guilt trips. It can also include less obvious forms such as opinions, assessments, diagnostics, and evaluations, all of which are simply different forms of judgment.

To become proficient at NVC and Emergency Empathy, it's crucial to understand what constitutes violent language and what doesn't. We will elaborate on this further in later chapters, and if the only takeaway you get from this book is this understanding, it'll be well worth the cover price.

WHY DO WE USE VIOLENT LANGUAGE?

In general, our use of violent language can be traced back to experiencing some form of fear. These forms might include:

- Fear of a certain behavior continuing or not continuing
- Fear for our safety or that of a loved one
- Fear of wasting time
- Fear of not getting what we want
- Fear of getting what we don't want
- Fear of what others will think

When we use violent language, such as calling someone a derogatory name, it's often done with the misguided hope that the humiliation will inspire them to change their behavior. It's rarely done in outright animosity with the intent to hurt. Instead, we may think that if they just hear this hurtful name and/or harsh criticism, they'll somehow recognize their behavior as wrong and decide to do better. At the moment, it seems logical.

The problem: This approach almost never works, and if it does, it often comes at the high cost of resentment and disconnection. More often, the other person gets triggered and lashes out with their own violent language. Hearing this, we too become triggered, which intensifies our response and fuels a cycle of escalation until it spirals into a full-blown argument with the potential to cause lasting damage to the relationship.

This type of interaction can happen in any relationship dynamic including friends, relatives, spouses, or even total strangers. Take parenting, for example. Parents want the best for their kids. But in the name of love, they can slip into using violent, forceful language or coercive tactics, believing it's justified if it "helps them learn." Although the intention may be positive, the outcome can often be disconnection and resentment. Yes, parents have a natural authority over young children, and sometimes firm intervention is necessary, especially in moments of danger. But using verbal force in everyday situations tends to backfire. It may lead to short-term compliance, but it rarely results in deeper connection. In general, verbal force leads children to comply out of fear rather than understanding.

NVC and Emergency Empathy offer us an alternative way to get the results we desire while building more connection. This works with people of all ages, including children barely old enough to speak. These methods honor the needs of both parties, as they work toward a win-win solution, a truly desirable outcome.

WHAT IS NONVIOLENT COMMUNICATION?

Nonviolent Communication is a set of understandings and guidelines that help:

- Set boundaries.
- Navigate sensitive topics.
- Resolve conflicts.
- Find sustainable, mutually satisfying solutions.

NVC builds trust and connection by encouraging communication that is both authentic and specific, while leaving judgments out entirely. It consists of four simple yet powerful steps that provide a clear pathway to address issues without assigning blame or implying someone is wrong or bad. Though each step may seem deceptively simple, they build upon each other in meaningful ways. We'll explore each in much greater detail in the following chapters, but for now, here are the four basic steps:

STEP 1: Bring attention to the issue using only observable facts.
STEP 2: Express how you authentically feel.
STEP 3: Express why you feel the way you do.
STEP 4: Make a specific request.

For example:

STEP 1: When I got home from work today, I noticed the air conditioner was set to 65 degrees.
STEP 2: I'm feeling a little frustrated . . .
STEP 3: . . . because I don't want another extremely high electric bill like last month, especially since nobody is home most of the day.
STEP 4: Would you mind if I program the AC so that it stays at 72 during the day?

The beauty of NVC lies in its simplicity and ability to navigate anything from the most mundane to the trickiest and most sensitive situations. Anyone can learn and apply this to great effect, as long as they're willing to embrace the fundamental principles.

EMERGENCY EMPATHY

While NVC can work amazingly well at helping resolve nearly any conflict, there is a very specific time when it tends to fall short. This is usually the precise moment you or the person you are talking with becomes triggered and overcome with strong negative emotions. NVC deals with logic and clear, pragmatic, solution-oriented steps. Unfortunately, in an emotionally charged interaction, these tend to be ignored in favor of more immediate impulses.

This is when Emergency Empathy steps in. It is the yin to NVC's yang, specifically designed to work when NVC reaches its limits. It can be extremely helpful in nearly any situation, but it is especially useful for de-escalating intense emotions.

Emergency Empathy's primary purpose is to rapidly build connection and help the other person feel calm by letting them know they've been heard and understood. By acknowledging their inner world and highlighting the issue they are experiencing, Emergency Empathy helps reduce tension while building connection and opening the door to a more constructive interaction.

In emotionally charged exchanges, conversations can quickly spiral, as people tend to stop listening to each other. Often, voices will rise and get harsh, with both sides repeating themselves more and more emphatically in an attempt to get their point across, and yet comprehension diminishes. This is because triggered people aren't fully listening anymore. So no matter how well you've made your point, they probably didn't hear it. It's the same from the other way around: If something has triggered you, you may be unable to fully hear what the other person is saying because you're stuck in your own sense of preservation.

Once someone shifts into fight-or-flight mode, they can no longer comprehend the nuances of what's being said. In fact, it is likely that everything said can and will be used against the speaker, whether they're using NVC or not. In most cases, the triggered party will either ignore the points entirely, insisting the speaker first understand their perspective, or they'll interpret the words in the most negative way possible. The triggered person often resorts to verbally violent tactics to get *the other person* triggered as well.

If one person remains calm while the other is triggered, there's still hope that peace can be found relatively soon. The problem is that anger spreads like wildfire, especially if the triggered party is using insults, lies, mischaracterizations, exaggerations, straw man tactics, and blame, all while raising their voice and using aggressive body language. Staying calm amid this intensity is incredibly challenging, but this is where Emergency Empathy truly shines. This simple technique cuts through the haze of fiery language and hurt feelings, piercing straight to the heart of the issue. Depending on the circumstances it might sound something like this: "Are you feeling upset because you haven't had a chance to fully tell your side of the story yet?"

If this is accurate and the triggered person realizes they've been heard and understood, they usually no longer feel the need to repeat themselves, speak in louder and louder tones, or use derogatory language. At this point, they will likely begin to calm down and become open to hearing what you'd like to express. I'll talk through this process in much more detail in the following chapters.

CONFLICT SUPPRESSION AND THE PAIN BODY

Many people believe it's better to keep their negative feelings to themselves in an effort to maintain peace. They might think they're being honorable, they're taking the high road, or even that their feelings don't actually matter. However, conflicts rarely disappear when ignored. In fact, the longer they're left unresolved, the more intense they tend to become. We saw this in the introduction, where my silence and my colleague's silence only built up tension until there was a near-relationship-ending blowup.

The truth is that conflict is both natural and inevitable. It's unrealistic to expect a life shared with others to be free of it. What one person sees as a treasure, another may view as trash; a compliment to one may feel like an insult to another. Even the same word with the same spelling can have multiple meanings. All of these factors—and many more—ensure that misunderstandings and conflicts will forever be a part of our lives.

But the gift of conflict lies in the opportunity it brings to strengthen our relationships. When a conflict has surfaced and been resolved, it often leads to a deeper feeling of connection and a more resilient bond. A relationship that's navigated through a disagreement is stronger than one that's never been tested. Any relationship that has learned to handle issues swiftly and thoroughly has the potential to endure for a lifetime, and this is what NVC and Emergency Empathy can provide.

Eckhart Tolle is an author and teacher whose wisdom has had a profound impact on my life. One of the concepts he teaches is the idea of a *pain body*. This concept has given me many insights, and I believe it can be particularly useful when learning Emergency Empathy and NVC. As I understand it, the pain body can be thought of as a collection of emotions that a person has suppressed throughout their lifetime. Every time we feel a negative emotion but choose to suppress it, that feeling doesn't just disappear. So where does it go?

According to Tolle, suppressed emotions gather with other suppressed feelings in our bodies to form something like an emotional parasite that feeds on similar negativities. Most of the time it lies dormant inside us, waiting for something to occur that will provide a negative emotion to feed on. Tolle compares it to a cat that's sleeping but always has one ear alert, listening for an opportunity to feed. Feeding the pain body occurs from not only strong negative emotions within us but also those around us.

An example of this occurred in my life years ago when I was waiting to talk with my girlfriend about something that was bothering me. I was more than a little upset, but I did my best to stay calm when I brought it up to her. She, on the other hand, was in the opposite mood, carefree and happy and not wanting to have a serious conversation. I grew increasingly annoyed, interpreting her cheerful attitude as indifference to something important to me. My tone shifted and my rising level of anger became clear. My language became critical and judgmental, and she soon became triggered as well.

Then something happened that struck me to my core and made me realize how profound and accurate Tolle's ideas about the pain body are: As soon as she got upset and raised her voice, my own frustration and anger instantly vanished. I was no longer upset at all. My bad attitude had disappeared as if it had never been there, and I found myself feeling oddly carefree and cheerful instead. I thought, *Wow! My pain body just fed on her pain body.* This realization left me feeling extremely ashamed. From that day on, I committed to staying aware of my pain body whenever it arises, doing everything in my power to resist and prevent myself from acting on its impulses.

When our pain body awakens or we're triggered (two ways of describing nearly the same thing), we often lose control of our emotions, showing our lowest self and taking the longest path to finding a win-win solution. This is how someone can be so loving and rational in one moment, and so hurtful and irrational in the next. Once the pain body recedes and calmness returns, we regain our senses and often feel embarrassed by our actions. But the damage is already done.

If we surrender control to our pain body, it will eagerly generate as much negative emotion as possible, within us and those around us, until it's full. It's a kind of temporary insanity making one believe yelling insults at someone they love is somehow a good idea. I can assure you, it never is. Though conflict is an inevitable part of life, conflict fueled by our suppressed emotions can create long-lasting scars on our relationships and rarely ends in a mutually beneficial resolution.

Awareness of our pain body and its habits, desires, and patterns can be helpful in mitigating the harm it causes. Understanding that everyone has a pain body can help us have empathy and avoid taking their words or actions too personally, especially when it's clear they're acting from a place of pain. Instead, simply focus on the tools and principles of NVC. These will bring much quicker, long-lasting results, and your pain body will have significantly less influence on your actions. For a deeper understanding of the pain body, I highly recommend exploring Tolle's books and videos.

The main push of this book is to help you understand and become proficient at the use of Emergency Empathy to bolster your connections and counteract the pain body response. Because this method is most effective when used in conjunction with NVC, the next chapter will first briefly give you the fundamentals before we fully dive into the practice.

2

Understanding the Core Tenets of NVC

MARSHALL ROSENBERG DEVELOPED the process of Nonviolent Communication in the late sixties and seventies after his experiences in the Detroit race riots and his work helping to desegregate schools in the American South. He formulated it by combining key communication principles from different Indigenous cultures, spiritual traditions, and modern psychology, weaving them together into a seamless and easy-to-understand process that has spread throughout the world. NVC has been successfully used countless times to resolve interpersonal conflicts all the way to mediating peace in conflict zones between countries.

At the heart of NVC are four core tenets: authenticity, nonjudgment, accountability, and specificity. Each plays a crucial role and must be deeply understood and wholeheartedly embraced to be successful at resolving conflicts. Let's explore what it means to incorporate these powerful concepts into our practice.

AUTHENTICITY

Being authentic means you are able to express your true feelings, admit what you honestly think or feel, and ask for what you truly desire. Being authentic while using NVC helps cut through the haze of vague language and quickly uncovers the heart of the matter. In contrast, inauthenticity takes the long and winding scenic route, often leaving people feeling frustrated, unheard, and misunderstood.

The more honest and authentic you are, the more likely others will be too. If you are anything other than authentic, then you're essentially telling some form of a lie, be it white, gray, or black. How can that be a good idea? When is a lie better than the truth? The truth lasts forever and never changes. It's profound and can be leaned upon at any time. Honesty leads to more honesty; lies lead to more lies.

Most people would agree that lying is better avoided, but what about sugarcoating? What about being "nice" or offering partial truths to protect someone else's feelings? It may feel safer to be vague, polite, or "nice" because these strategies are less likely to ruffle feathers, but they are also less likely to result in meaningful progress.

For instance, you may say you're "slightly annoyed" when you're actually angry, or you may tell your partner you're upset because you wanted them to be on time when the real issue is that you're uncomfortable with the person they were spending time with. In an NVC context, these half-truths lead to distrust, disconnection, and missed opportunities. In the case of the above example, while you may get your partner to promise to be more punctual, your true issue will remain unaddressed. What have you really accomplished? How will you feel at the end of the conversation? What will happen the next time your partner spends time with that person and remains oblivious to your true feelings? Most likely your response will be even more intense and so will the ensuing interaction. Remember, the pain body stores these unexpressed negative emotions, waiting for the next opportunity to surface and often creates a much larger conflict that could have been avoided.

It's much easier to find a win-win and sustainable solution to an issue when you're authentic about what's bothering you and how you truly feel. This doesn't mean it will be easy; in fact, it can often be hard and messy. But in the long run, authenticity will always be the more efficient path. When you're authentic, especially with your current emotions, it resonates with those around you. Your words and body language will be effortlessly congruent, and this builds trust and connection. When they're incongruent, it inevitably leads to mistrust and disconnection.

Some people find it difficult to admit to feeling negative emotions such as anger, annoyance, or sadness. This difficulty often stems from the vulnerability required to express these emotions, particularly when taking full ownership of them without blaming anyone else. For example:

- "I feel sad."
- "I feel angry."
- "I feel annoyed."
- "I feel anxious."

How does it feel to say these words out loud? Do you experience discomfort? Shame? Many people worry that being direct about any emotions other than joy might come across as confrontational. However, when you follow all the tenets of NVC, it is unlikely to be as offensive as you might fear. What most people find offensive is being blamed for another's negative emotions or being told they're bad or wrong. For example:

- "*You're* making me sad."
- "I'm angry because of what *you* just said."
- "*You're* annoying me."

Each one of these statements implies the other person is doing something wrong and is responsible for causing the negative emotions in the speaker. Expressing how you authentically feel and what you truly desire should never contain blame or judgments if you're following the principles of NVC correctly. Therefore, it's much easier for someone to hear your true feelings and thoughts than you might initially expect.

NONJUDGMENT

Understanding judgment is essential to communication, yet there's a lot of confusion surrounding the topic due to the various meanings of the word. There are actually four distinctions: legal judgments, divine judgments, discerning judgments, and condemning judgments. The first two types are pretty self-explanatory. One pertains to judgments from a legal judge in court and the other to judgment from God.

The latter two, though, often get confused. *Discerning judgment* involves using factual information to understand the deeper truth of a situation without any sense of condemnation. *Condemning judgment* involves forming an opinion that assigns value—or lack of—to someone or something. Anytime we imply that someone or something is "wrong" or "bad," we are engaging in condemning judgment. The same applies when we offer our opinion, evaluation, assessment, or diagnosis, if the end result is implying that someone is bad or wrong. In this book, we're going to focus specifically on condemning judgment.

When working to resolve a conflict using NVC, it is essential to focus on the facts. Our personal judgments and opinions are far less helpful and often complicate the process. Most conflicts are much easier to resolve if we either keep our condemning judgments to ourselves or, even better, eliminate them altogether. For many of us, it can be very humbling to realize how frequently we judge others directly and in our minds. I know it was for me. When we judge and condemn someone, it implies that we see ourselves as superior and as having moral authority. Yet the world is infinitely complex. Without a complete understanding of a person, situation, or topic, our judgments are only guesses, often completely incorrect and, at best, only partially accurate.

During a conflict, when people are on a hair trigger, condemning someone or their actions almost always escalates the intensity, creating greater separation with no actual benefit aside from a fleeting ego boost for the morally superior "judge." If we imply that someone is bad or wrong, it also implies that we are not. This is one of the reasons this behavior is so prevalent. Most people don't respond well to being told they're "bad" or "wrong." Most people react by becoming defensive and lashing out with their own condemning judgment, igniting further cycles of conflict. Using NVC, there's always a way to express the underlying sentiment without any condemning judgment.

Let's look at an example. Instead of saying, "You're acting ridiculous right now" (judgment), try, "I don't understand why you're acting this way" (a factual statement with no condemnation). Rather than declaring, "He's a terrible person" (judgment), say, "He has been in and out of jail for violent crimes since high school"(a factual statement that can be verified). These alternatives convey the point without unnecessary provocation, providing less fodder for others to get triggered by. In general:

- **FACTS** are clear, measurable, and verifiable.
- **JUDGMENTS** are vague, unverifiable, and unmeasurable.

Judgments, such as . . .

- "He's a jerk."
- "She's useless."
- "He's dumb."
- "She's lazy."

. . . mean different things to different people and can never be definitively proven. In contrast, facts provide concrete, verifiable information. Let's compare the two.

JUDGMENT: "It's too cold in here."
FACT: "It's 65 degrees in the house right now."

JUDGMENT: "The movie was way too long."
FACT: "The movie was two hours and forty-five minutes long."

JUDGMENT: "This band sounds terrible."
FACT: "The lead singer is singing out of key."

JUDGMENT: "He's untrustworthy."
FACT: "I caught him lying to me three different times in the past few weeks."

Speaking in facts helps to discern the situation with clarity, while judgments oversimplify and exaggerate. Judgments are always open to interpretation and can never be fully verified. This lack of objectivity is prime fuel for argumentative disagreements.

Before learning Nonviolent Communication, I believed that labeling people and situations with my opinions and judgments was actually beneficial. I thought it would protect me, offer insights, and help me understand the world better. Through practicing NVC, I discovered the opposite is true. Instead of creating understanding and connection, judging creates barriers and oversimplifications. One reason for this is because as soon as we label something, it's as if we're mentally putting it inside a box where we no longer have to be present with it. It then becomes easy to fall into the trap of believing our opinions are facts. Phrases such as "This is good," "That's bad," "They're untrustworthy," or "He's selfish" create rigid categories that prevent us from being present with and understanding the complexities of the situation or person.

While labels can occasionally help clarify or simplify, they also tend to reduce things to a single word or phrase, which almost always oversimplifies, so we miss out on the nuanced truth. We miss out on the true reality of the ever-changing landscapes of life and human interaction.

I'm not suggesting that people should never express an opinion. Rather, when practicing NVC or Emergency Empathy, avoid expressing unsolicited opinions and instead speak in observable facts as much as possible. This approach allows you to make your point in a much more powerful and relatable way while mitigating the risk of the other person becoming triggered. If someone asks for your opinion, it's perfectly fine to share it, as long as you make it clear that it's an opinion, not a fact. Prefacing with phrases such as

- In my opinion . . .
- I think . . .
- From my perspective . . .

helps to maintain clarity in the conversation, ensuring that your perspective is understood as subjective rather than absolute.

There's a significant difference between saying "You're doing it wrong" and "In my opinion, you're doing it wrong," or between "That's not a good idea" and "I don't think that's a good idea."

The first implies that you're the authority on the subject and your view is an indisputable fact, which shuts down further discussion. The other admits this is just an opinion and no more valid than anybody else's opinion—a much more honest way to communicate. These small but powerful adjustments can make a world of difference if you're looking to avoid unproductive conflicts.

Of course, there are situations where opinions, judgments, and criticisms are completely natural and even necessary. Art critics are paid for their opinions. Coaches must provide performance feedback. However, these contexts are outside the scope of this book. Here we're focusing on conflicts within interpersonal relationships. This is where it's crucial to eliminate all opinions and judgments, not just verbally but also in your thoughts. If you hold strong negative opinions about someone but never express them verbally, chances are they will leak out one way or another through your word choice, tone, or body language. Unspoken negativity tends to manifest in subtle, nonverbal cues, which can often be more detrimental than expressing it outright. I highly recommend eliminating judgmental thoughts and words as much as possible and instead speaking and thinking in factual ways. This can take a while to achieve, but the more you practice NVC, the more this will naturally occur—as long as you accept the underlying principles. Judgmental thoughts tend to have a certain feeling to them. The less you allow them in, the more noticeable they are when they appear.

I've worked with people who are going through a difficult time with a loved one, and as they tell me what's going on, I always make sure they speak without using judgments and opinions, even though the person they're talking about is not present. Words are powerful; they shape how we perceive reality. Opinions change like the weather, but facts stay the same. When we speak and think in facts, we're grounded in reality. When we speak and think in opinions and judgments, we are floating in an ever-changing and oversimplified fantasy that paints one person as a victim and the other as a villain. This distorts reality, and the next interaction with this supposed "villain" will likely be tainted by these judgmental thoughts.

Here are a few more examples of how to shape your opinions and judgments into factual statements:

OPINION: "My ex treated me very badly."
FACT: "My ex cheated on me three times."

OPINION: "My ex was very stingy."
FACT: "My ex refused to leave tips of more than 10 percent when we would go out to eat."

OPINION: "My ex doesn't know how to love."
FACT: "My ex never once told me they loved me."

A key point to remember is that speaking with judgments creates unnecessary fuel for conflicts with little to no benefit. Speaking in observable facts allows you to express yourself authentically while reducing the risks of an unproductive argument.

Internal Facts

There is another category of facts that I refer to as *internal facts*. These are true statements that can only be verified by the speaker. For example, your feelings are facts that cannot be measured or confirmed by anyone else, yet they remain facts. Your preferences, desires, and thoughts also fall into this category. For example:

OPINION: "He's a reckless driver."
FACT: "He's been in three car accidents in the past few years."
INTERNAL FACT: "I don't feel comfortable riding with him."

OPINION: "Your skirt is too short."
FACT: "Your skirt is six inches above your knees."
INTERNAL FACT: "I would prefer it if you'd wear a longer skirt."

OPINION: "Your bedroom is a mess."
FACT: "Your bed is unmade, there's garbage on the floor, and there are dirty dishes on your desk."
INTERNAL FACT: "I don't enjoy spending time in your room when it's in this state."

The essence of these statements are the same, but by speaking in facts instead of opinions, they have a much better chance of being received in a productive way. With practice, this approach becomes almost second nature.

ACCOUNTABILITY

Taking responsibility for how we feel at all times is absolutely essential to being consistently effective at NVC. No matter the circumstances, it's always our interpretation of events that shapes how we feel, making us ultimately responsible for our feelings.

For instance, if a date cancels at the last moment, it might seem natural to feel anger or sadness and assume the person who canceled is to blame. After all, if they hadn't canceled, you wouldn't feel disappointed, right? But in reality, it's your interpretation of the event that generates these feelings. The same event could lead to very different feelings, depending on your perspective. If you didn't want to go on the date, or if you had a busy schedule the following morning, you might even feel relief. Though the canceled date can be considered the catalyst for your feelings, it's not the cause. You are ultimately responsible for how you interpret something, so you are ultimately responsible for how you feel about that thing.

Consider a more extreme scenario. You catch a teenager breaking into your car. A common response might be anger or outrage due to all the hassle and expenses this will cost you. However, if instead you consider the hardships this teen must have had to be committing acts like this, you might feel sad knowing this is really just a cry for help. You might even feel excited if you choose to see this as an opportunity to help someone in need. It's even possible you could feel all three emotions, one after the other, as you process all the angles. Whatever the actual reason might be for the break-in, your perspective can alter the way you feel about the perpetrator and give you valuable practice in nonjudgmental thinking.

One more example: Imagine you're sitting on a train and the passenger next to you is noisily eating with their mouth open while you're trying to read a complicated book. A common reaction might be annoyance. Once again, though this would be stimulated by the passenger, the real reason you feel annoyed would still be coming from your own values and expectations. If good manners are an important value to you, then you would likely find eating with your mouth open annoying. The real reason you feel this way is the underlying belief and not the action of the passenger. If you came from a culture where eating with your mouth open was common, you would likely feel different.

There are countless scenarios, each stimulating different thoughts and values that would produce an equally diverse range of reactions. Imagine if the passenger is a celebrity you admire, and instead of annoyance you think it's fascinating, finding it endearing that even celebrities have quirks. Or maybe you're excited because it gives you an opportunity to practice a meditation technique that teaches how to block out aggravating sounds. How you feel always depends on how you frame the situation, the thoughts you have around it, and the values you hold. This is why it's crucial to take responsibility for your feelings at all times and avoid blaming others, whether directly or indirectly. This is one of the biggest challenges many students have.

When we place responsibility for our emotions on others, we also inadvertently surrender our personal power. If our internal emotional state is always at the mercy of the world around us, then we can never truly be in control of ourselves. We will constantly be a victim to the circumstances of our environment, and we can have no emotional stability. By fully taking responsibility for our feelings, we maintain the power to manage our reactions and adjust our perspectives, putting us in control of our emotional state.

Subtle Implications

It's crucial to meticulously avoid even the slightest implication that someone else is to blame for your feelings. This requires diligence, as it's easy to unintentionally place responsibility on others with common phrases such as:

- "It makes me sad that you didn't say goodbye."
- "I'm annoyed because you're so late."
- "I'm upset because you left the kitchen a mess."

Each of these statements suggests that the other person is responsible for how you feel and subtly implies that they're bad and wrong. A correct way to express these same sentiments from an NVC perspective might sound like:

- "I feel sad because saying goodbye is important to me."
- "I feel annoyed because I really like punctuality."
- "I'm upset because I value cleanliness."

These statements use only facts and feelings without blame or implications of wrongdoing. This brings the responsibility back to ourselves by making "I" statements as opposed to "you" statements. This shift may seem subtle, but it can be the difference between a successful conversation and one that leads to defensiveness or conflict.

On the flip side, it's also important to recognize that you're never responsible for how someone else feels, whether it's their happiness or sadness. You may be a catalyst, much like the teen who broke into the car, but you cannot control or dictate their emotional response. This doesn't mean it's a good idea to go around being abusive and impolite, especially if you want to live a low-conflict life filled with great relationships. Negative behaviors will inevitably arouse negative consequences. Personally, even though I know I'm not responsible for how anyone else feels, I strive to ensure my actions serve as a catalyst for positive emotions rather than negative ones.

SPECIFICITY

The more I teach NVC, the more I recognize how important specificity is in getting consistent results. Many times, when one of my students is facing a particularly challenging situation that seems stagnant, the solution often lies in using greater specificity. Specific questions get specific answers. Specific requests yield specific results. In contrast, vague language produces vague and unproductive results. For example:

VAGUE: "Would you be willing to clean up more around the house?"

At first glance, this might seem like a reasonable request. Yet how much more cleaning are we talking about? Is it 30 percent more or 10 percent more? Even 1 percent more would technically fulfill the request. How would it be measured? How would anyone know if the request was fulfilled? How often does this need to occur to be considered "more"? The reality is that even if the person agrees, nobody truly understands what was just agreed upon. At the moment, it might seem like something was accomplished, but more than likely it will not be sufficient for a long-term, sustainable solution.

Instead, a specific request might sound like:

- "Would you be willing to vacuum the living room twice a week?"
- "As soon as you come home from school on Mondays, will you sweep the kitchen and take out the trash?"
- "Will you spend at least fifteen minutes a day cleaning up around the house?"

These are clear, measurable requests that leave little room for misinterpretation. Let's look at a couple of other comparisons:

VAGUE: "Would you be willing to be more respectful?"
SPECIFIC: "Would you be willing to stop using curse words around me?"

VAGUE: "Would you be willing to put more energy into our relationship?"
SPECIFIC: "Would you be willing to schedule a date night each week where we spend some quality one-on-one time together?"

Specificity is not only important when making requests. It's also helpful when revealing how you feel or what is bothering you. Many people shy away from using a high level of specificity with these topics because, unlike ambiguous language, it leaves no place to hide for either the speaker or the listener. Specificity is very revealing, and this is one reason why it's so powerful but also so scary.

This is an easy-to-overlook principle, but I highly recommend that you keep it present in your mind, especially when you're feeling frustrated while attempting NVC. It should be one of your go-to strategies at the first signs of trouble. As soon as it seems like the conversation is going in circles or the person you're speaking with starts showing signs of restlessness, boredom, confusion, or glazed-over eyes, a little specificity might quickly change the course of the conversation for the better.

We will go deeper into these concepts as the book progresses, but for now I just want to plant the seeds. The sooner these are fully embraced, the quicker you will become proficient at resolving conflicts efficiently and consistently.

3

Starting Your NVC Dialogue

WHILE EMERGENCY EMPATHY is designed for rapidly building connection and de-escalating intense situations, NVC is used for setting boundaries and finding long-term, sustainable, win-win solutions. Each method can be effective on its own, but their true power emerges when they're used in tandem. Together, there is no problem that these techniques can't vastly improve.

The true starting point of NVC occurs the moment you become aware something is bothering you or someone else. Once this occurs, it's time to begin the four steps that we saw in chapter 1:

STEP 1: Bring attention to the issue using observable facts while leaving out all judgments.
STEP 2: Express how you authentically feel without suggesting someone else is responsible for it.
STEP 3: Express why you feel the way you do, which always ties back to a value, desire, preference, or need you have.
STEP 4: Make a specific request that has the potential to lead to a win-win solution.

These steps form the foundation of NVC and will serve as a guide while we delve deeper into the practice of Emergency Empathy. Let's look at an example that will provide a clear and practical illustration of how to apply the four steps of Nonviolent Communication in a real-life scenario.

Christine walks into the kitchen and sees the garbage is full to the point of overflowing. She instantly feels annoyed. Her husband, Henry, is currently sitting on the couch watching ESPN, even though he'd previously agreed to take out the garbage whenever it becomes full.

CHRISTINE

(PRECURSOR)

Honey, can I talk with you about something?

HENRY

Sure.

CHRISTINE

(STEP 1)

I can see the garbage hasn't been emptied,
and it's so full the lid won't properly close.

(No judgment, just observable facts)

(STEP 2)

I'm feeling frustrated . . .

(Authentic feeling, clearly stated with no blame)

(STEP 3)

. . . because having a clean kitchen is important to me,
especially when I'm cooking.

*(Taking responsibility for her feelings,
connecting them to her own values and preferences)*

(STEP 4)

Would you be willing to take out the garbage
in the next few minutes?

(A request that is both achievable and specific)

This is a basic example of a Nonviolent Communication interaction. Each step, while seemingly simple, can be challenging to execute correctly. Even minor missteps in phrasing can derail the process, leading to unintended conflicts. In fact, I often compare practicing NVC to walking through a minefield. Everything can feel calm and straightforward until you take one wrong step, and then, out of nowhere, a huge explosion. In NVC, this one wrong step typically involves introducing judgment, blame, or an implication that the other person is wrong and bad in some way. Any of these can easily trigger the person you're speaking with, making it much more difficult to find a win-win solution.

STEP 1: NAMING THE ISSUE

Sometimes identifying the issue in step 1 is fairly straightforward, as demonstrated in the trash scenario. Other times we might feel annoyed without immediately being aware of what's bothering us. It could be something that was said, something left unsaid, the tone it was said in, or the uncertainty in what they mean. For instance, Christine could have responded sarcastically instead of using NVC when she saw Henry watching sports while the garbage was overflowing.

CHRISTINE

Having fun?

If she followed up by slamming cupboards and drawers while muttering under her breath, Henry might start to feel a bit triggered, and an NVC statement from him might sound like this:

HENRY

(PRECURSOR)

Hi, honey, hope your day went well.

(STEP 1)

I'm not sure what you mean by that question.

(This would fall under the category of internal fact. It's only observable to him, yet it's a fact that he's not sure what she means and serves the purpose of bringing attention to the statement he's having an issue with.)

(STEP 2)

. . . and I'm feeling a little anxious . . .

(Authentic feeling without blame)

(STEP 3)

. . . because I prefer a more direct style of communication.

(Expressing that the reason he is upset is his own preference)

(STEP 4)

Would you be willing to clarify what you meant when you said, "Having fun?"

(Specific request that is achievable)

Every step is authentic, spoken in natural-sounding language and void of any judgments, blame, or implications of wrongdoing. This gives them the best chance to find a mutually satisfying solution to the tension while avoiding escalation into an argument

Common Challenges of Step 1

One common challenge is avoiding directly or indirectly implying that the other person is wrong and bad in any way. Even a subtle suggestion of this will instantly make the conversation far more difficult. Here's an example of an incorrect way to approach step 1 using the overflowing-trash scenario.

CHRISTINE

Are you ever gonna empty the trash?

While this statement fulfills the task of bringing attention to the full trash, it also implies that it *should* have been emptied already, suggesting that Henry is wrong for not doing so. These implications immediately increase the chances of the interaction becoming tense and adversarial.

This is one of the most crucial concepts to embrace. It's vital in each step of NVC as well as during Emergency Empathy. Anytime you imply someone is wrong and bad, there's a host of other implications that come along with it, such as:

- You're morally superior to them.
- You're a victim of their actions.
- They're responsible for your pain.
- They're a problem.
- You're the judge of what is right and wrong.
- They need to change.
- You don't need to change.

This might sound extreme, but it reflects a fundamental truth of human interactions: Communication is a complex and multilayered endeavor. Every statement you make will have many implications. Any negative implications, however subtle, will likely be immediately understood by the other person, and more times than not, their response will not be pleasant. They will often become defensive and start making statements that imply you also are wrong and bad, and now an argument is much harder to avoid.

If you want consistent results, it's imperative to stop implying anyone is bad and wrong at all costs. I can't stress this enough. It doesn't matter if a hundred out of a hundred people agree that the other person is at fault. There is no benefit, from a conflict resolution standpoint, to saying it out loud. What matters is speaking authentically, finding a win-win solution, and growing closer in the process.

Another common challenge is avoiding exaggerations. It is best to be as accurate as you can in your wording when bringing attention to an issue. Using extreme language to grab attention will only increase the odds of the other person becoming triggered and a solution that is much harder to find. Words such as *never*, *always*, and *ever* are also better avoided. These words add intensity and impact but often stretch the truth, as few situations are that absolute. For example:

CHRISTINE

The kitchen is a disaster zone.

This is an exaggeration and a judgment that implies Henry is bad and wrong as well as all the other implications listed above. Even if most people would agree that the kitchen is a mess, it's still more effective to use observable facts than blanket judgmental statements, if what you want is a quick and painless resolution.

Here is an example of doing step 1 using only observable facts:

CHRISTINE

The trash is overflowing, and the sink is full of dirty dishes.

This brings attention to the catalyst of the issue while containing no judgments or exaggerations.

STEP 2: FEELINGS

In step 1 we addressed the facts of the issue without judgment. Now in step 2 we reveal how we currently feel. The key to step 2 is keeping it simple and authentic. The first thing to understand is the difference between a real feeling and a faux feeling. Real feelings describe an internal emotional state, while faux feelings imply something has been done to you externally. Faux feelings often include a series of negative judgments toward the other person while not actually explaining how you feel.

REAL FEELINGS: Sad, lonely, scared, upset, concerned, frustrated, annoyed, angry, stressed, worried, confused, terrified, tired, irritated, anxious, impatient, uncomfortable, unsafe, grumpy, unstable, ashamed, jealous, hopeless, afraid, bored, resentful, insecure, overwhelmed

FAUX FEELINGS: Disrespected, abandoned, ignored, abused, mistreated, unappreciated, unloved, used, ganged up on, left out, betrayed, neglected, cheated, insulted, manipulated, violated, judged, bullied, rejected, oppressed

Faux feelings sound like real feelings except they imply that:

- Someone did something to you.
- Whoever did this to you is wrong and bad for doing it.
- They are the cause of your pain.
- You are a victim of their bad actions.

For example, when someone says, "I feel disrespected by you," what they're really saying is:

- "You're being disrespectful." (judgment)
- "You shouldn't have been disrespectful to me." (judgment)
- "You're bad and wrong." (judgment)

- "I'm an innocent victim." (judgment)
- "You should change." (judgment)

One of the biggest challenges in tense communications is that even a single poorly phrased sentence can dramatically shift the entire tone of a conversation. When someone uses faux feelings, they're often unaware of the deeper implications behind their words. Most likely they're not being malicious and out to cause harm. It's just that this is how most of us have been taught to communicate. Expressing genuine feelings requires vulnerability, especially when those feelings are considered negative. Accusing someone of mistreating us and making it sound like a feeling is far easier and requires no vulnerability, which is why this is so common and challenging to overcome. Yet it is absolutely essential to avoid.

Even highly educated therapists and psychologists can fall into this pattern of communication. In fact, many of the psychologists I've worked with over the years were astonished to realize they hadn't been taught the fundamentals of NVC and Emergency Empathy during their formal training, especially after witnessing just how powerful and effective these methods can be.

All of the faux feelings essentially imply the same set of judgments. Let's look at another example. Saying "I feel neglected" implies:

- Someone neglected them.
- The neglect shouldn't have happened.
- The person who neglected them is wrong and bad.
- The one who feels neglected is a victim of the other's wrongdoing.
- The person who neglected them should change because only bad people neglect others.

This is quite a heavy load, all wrapped in what at the surface seems like a vulnerable expression of feelings. This is one of the land mines you can step on that may completely sidetrack the conversation. When someone is on the receiving end of a faux feeling, they often experience an immediate sense of injustice and instinctively want to defend themselves with their own aggressive tactics, which can quickly escalate into a full-blown argument.

Speaking nonviolently demands a high level of self-awareness and meticulousness in word choice. In the beginning it can feel daunting, but over time it gets much easier. To express the same sentiment as earlier and stay in alignment with NVC principles, instead of using the word *neglected*, you might use one of these options:

- "I feel lonely because I would like to spend more time with you."
- "I feel sad because I want to have more connection with you."
- "I feel upset because it's important to me to spend quality time regularly with you."

These alternatives contain only facts and are void of all judgments or blame. This makes them much easier to hear and much more likely to result in a positive outcome that builds connection. It can also make them harder to say.

Any feeling that implies someone is doing something that is wrong and harmful to you is not a real feeling. It's a faux feeling and a judgment. A feeling should contain zero implications of blame, judgments, or wrongdoing from another. To test if it's a real feeling, ask yourself, *Am I blaming anyone else? Am I judging anyone else? Could I feel this way alone on a desert island?* If a feeling requires another person to be involved, then it's most likely not a genuine feeling but a judgment disguised as one.

However, it's not always black and white, because language is nuanced. Words often have multiple meanings, sometimes completely different and other times only subtly different. For example, *annoyed* could be argued to imply someone is doing something annoying to you. However, you can definitely feel annoyed alone on a desert island. It really depends on the context.

Common Challenges of Step 2: I Feel As If . . .

A common habit to avoid that's extremely widespread is using feeling statements that begin with phrases such as "I feel as if . . ." or "I feel like . . ." The reason to avoid this is because whatever comes next is always going to be a judgment disguised as a feeling, implying the same underlying messages: *You are wrong and bad, I'm a victim, and you should change.* This type of phrasing is deeply ingrained in our modern-day vernacular. Here are some common examples:

- "I feel as if you don't care."
- "I feel like you're not listening to me."
- "I feel as if you're judging me."
- "I feel like you're not being honest."
- "I feel like this conversation is going nowhere."

This pattern of language can continue in endless variations. While these statements might sound like expressions of feeling, in reality they're all judgments. There's no actual feeling being conveyed in them at all.

We often speak this way because by framing a judgment as a feeling, it carries an extra air of authority or "higher truth." The implication becomes "It's not me saying it; it's my intuition or a higher power." This not only absolves the speaker of responsibility for the statement but also implies that it's a factual statement, which would be pointless to disagree with. Real feelings should be able to be expressed with one word:

- "I feel sad."
- "I feel upset."
- "I feel lonely."

If it takes more than one word, it's probably another judgment instead of a feeling.

The proper way to express "I feel as if . . ." or "I feel like . . ." statements from an NVC context is to replace the word *feel* with the word *think*. This is a more honest and accurate way to convey these sentiments:

- "I think you don't care."
- "I don't think you're listening to me."
- "I think you're judging me."
- "I think you're a dishonest person."
- "I don't think this conversation is going anywhere."

Alternatively, you can use "In my opinion . . ." or "From my perspective . . ." The crucial aspect is that you are phrasing your opinion as an opinion and not trying to disguise it as a feeling. This means you're taking full accountability for the thought and admitting it is based on nothing but your own beliefs and perceptions. This is what it means to be impeccable with your word.

This principle isn't just for structured NVC or Emergency Empathy; it enhances all types of communication. I encourage you to gradually eliminate using the phrases "I feel as if . . ." or "I feel like . . ." from your thoughts and everyday conversations. It takes courage to state opinions as opinions, and in the process, you may find yourself expressing fewer of them. Though it's common and may take time to unlearn, doing so will profoundly benefit your NVC journey. One of the greatest gifts I've received from using NVC is expressing my unsolicited opinions far less often. Life is much more peaceful this way.

As you can see, despite the simplicity of using observable facts and expressing your authentic feelings, there are many ways to do these steps incorrectly. Learning NVC is a process and most likely won't occur overnight, so allow yourself some grace as you learn to integrate this way of speaking into your life. The key points to remember are:

- Never imply someone is wrong or bad in any way.
- Use authentic one-word feelings.
- Avoid faux feelings.
- Avoid starting sentences with "I feel as if . . ." or "I feel like . . ."
- Avoid expressing judgments and opinions unless you phrase them as your opinion.

4

Identifying Values and Requests

In this chapter, we'll explore the final two steps of Nonviolent Communication. Like the first two, these steps are straightforward in principle but filled with opportunities for common mistakes. I'll highlight the key pitfalls to watch for and conclude with clear examples to bring each point to life.

STEP 3: VALUES

Once you've brought attention to an issue using observable facts and expressed how you genuinely feel, it's time for step 3: explaining why you feel the way you do.

This step is often overlooked but crucial to complete because it helps the other person understand where you're coming from and helps build empathy. Just as importantly, it shows that you're not blaming them for how you feel, which makes it much easier for them to listen without becoming defensive. In step 3, it's important to make it abundantly clear that your feelings arise from your own thoughts, values, desires, needs, or preferences and not from what the other person has said or done. This isn't about being nice or sugarcoating the situation; it's about being accurate and impeccable with our words. Let's look at an example to illustrate this idea.

John has an employee, Sam, who is thirty minutes late to a very important meeting. The first three steps of NVC, when done correctly by John, might sound like this:

JOHN

(STEP 1)

Sam, you're thirty minutes late . . .

(Observable fact, no judgment)

(STEP 2)

. . . and I'm feeling frustrated . . .

(Authentic feeling)

(STEP 3)

. . . because punctuality from my employees is important to me.

Or:

. . . because my time is very valuable to me.

Or:

. . . . because I prefer not to repeat myself.

These are correctly phrased step 3 statements. They don't point a finger at Sam by starting with "You . . .," and they don't include any judgments, blame, threats, or guilt trips. Instead, they focus on John's values and preferences, minimizing the chance that Sam gets defensive.

In contrast, incorrect step 3 statements might have sounded like:

(STEP 3—INCORRECT)

. . . because you're wasting everyone's time.

Or:

. . . because you're forcing me to have to repeat myself.

Or:

. . . because you obviously have no respect for your job.

Each of these statements are incorrectly phrased from an NVC point of view because they all start with "you" statements that blame Sam for how John feels and imply that Sam is somehow "bad and wrong" for being late. These will likely build resentment and loss of connection with Sam unnecessarily.

Let's use another example. Julie and Michael, a married couple, are having a conversation about politics when Michael raises his voice and the intensity begins to rapidly escalate.

MICHAEL

Look! I'm tired of this conversation. If you want to vote for a complete idiot, be my guest! I couldn't care less!

JULIE

(STEP 1)

Honey, when we're talking to each other and raising our voices . . .

(Observable facts without judgment)

(STEP 2)

. . . I feel sad . . .

(Authentic one-word feeling)

(STEP 3)

. . . because it's important to me for us to be able to discuss our differences without raising our voices.

Or:

. . . because I prefer to not be spoken to in that way.

Or:

. . . because I really value the ability to discuss our differences in a civil way.

These are correct step 3 statements because they honestly express why she feels the way she does without any blame, judgment, or implications of wrongdoing. She feels the way she does due to her values and preferences.

Here are some incorrect examples:

(STEP 3—INCORRECT)

. . . because you're being extremely rude.

Or:

. . . because you're losing your temper again.

Or:

. . . because you're acting like a child.

Each of these incorrect examples contains judgments and implications of wrongdoing and blame him for how she feels. Michael is likely to get more triggered and use violent language to defend himself, which will—more often than not—increase the feelings of disconnection between them and result in an argument.

The key point in step 3 is to remember that *we are always responsible for how we feel* because our emotions are shaped by our own preferences, values, and thoughts. If we change any of these, our feelings about the situation will change as well. Ultimately it's our internal perspective, not the external circumstances, that determines how we feel, and this must be clear in how we phrase step 3. Never start with a "you" statement. Instead, we should refer to what's important to us—our values, preferences, and needs.

STEP 4: THE SPECIFIC REQUEST

Now that you've brought attention to the issue using observable facts (step 1), expressed how you authentically feel (step 2), and explained why you feel that way (step 3), it is time for step 4, the specific request. This is what all the previous steps have been building toward. Each step is designed to create connection, understanding, and empathy so that this last step has the greatest potential to bring forth a win-win solution. Like all the steps, it's relatively simple, but there's a bit of nuance to it and many ways to do it incorrectly.

Request, Don't Demand

The first key concept to successfully execute step 4 is to ensure you're making a request as opposed to a demand. The main difference is that a request can be declined without fear of punishment, while a demand cannot. A demand is essentially a threat that implies, *Do this or bad things will happen.* From an NVC perspective, this is considered a violent tactic. If someone refuses your request and you react with anger, then it was actually a demand all along, no matter how nicely it was worded or how gentle your tone.

If someone refuses your request, the proper response is to think of another potential solution. If they keep refusing your requests, then at a certain point it's okay to ask if they have their own idea for a potential solution. At that point, if they refuse to offer any potential solutions, then there's probably a deeper issue at hand, yet to be addressed.

Specificity

The second detail to focus on is specificity. As we discussed in chapter 2, vague requests often sound promising, but the reality is they will almost never lead to long-term, sustainable solutions. A vague request could be "Would you be willing to . . .

- . . . be more helpful around the house?"
- . . . clean up more?"
- . . . be nicer to me?"
- . . . be more respectful."
- . . . be more of a team player?"
- . . . take better care of yourself?"
- . . . try harder?"

The problem with these requests is that they don't clearly define the parameters. If you ask someone to "be more respectful," nobody really knows what that means. How will it be measured? Who will be the judge? No doubt, each person will have their own internal definition of what "be more respectful" means, but how likely is it to be the same for two different people? The potential for this to become an issue again is high.

In contrast, a specific request might sound like "Would you be willing to . . .

- . . . mow the lawn twice a month?"
- . . . vacuum the house once a week?"
- . . . ask me how my day was when I get home from work?"
- . . . ask your coworkers if they need any help at least once a day?"
- . . . start doing intermittent fasting?"

These requests are clearly defined, and the person being asked knows what is expected of them. It will be obvious whether it's done or not as time passes. This is how real progress gets done. *Specific requests yield specific results*, while vague requests tend to lead to vague, unsatisfactory outcomes.

Achievability

The third key aspect to consider for your request is ensuring the ask is achievable. Some requests, while not impossible, are so unlikely to happen based on a single request that it becomes almost pointless to ask. An unrealistic request might be "Would you be willing to . . .

- . . . quit drinking?"
- . . . quit smoking?"
- . . . stop fighting with your sister?"
- . . . stop being so sensitive?"
- . . . stop being late?"
- . . . stop getting so angry?"

These behaviors are often part of deeply rooted emotional and psychological patterns that can almost never be turned off at a moment's notice. The key is to focus on progress, not instant perfection. Complex issues aren't likely to be solved in an instant, and they don't need to be. What's important is to be moving in the right direction. Here are some examples of achievable requests: "Would you be willing to . . .

- . . . start going to AA meetings?"
- . . . start using a nicotine patch?"
- . . . come to me first if you feel upset with your sister?"
- . . . start seeing a therapist?"
- . . . call me if you know you're going to be more than five minutes late?"
- . . . read this book on anger management?"

These requests are realistic, clear, and measurable, and you'll know whether or not they've been done. While they may not completely resolve the issue right away, that's not the immediate goal.

That's the long-term goal. The immediate goal is to make progress in the right direction. This is a realistic expectation and important to remember when making requests.

Three Types of Requests

The final aspect to consider is that there are three types of requests in NVC: action-based, clarity-based, and connection-based.

An action-based request involves a clear, action-oriented activity, such as taking out the trash, cleaning a room, doing the dishes, or working out. It can also involve stopping an activity, such as cursing inside the house, showing up late without calling ahead, smoking, or drinking. Examples of action-based requests include:

- "Would you be willing to mow the lawn today?"
- "Will you agree to start going to the gym twice a week?"
- "Would you start washing your dishes within one hour of finishing your meal?"

A clarity-based request seeks to understand why something has or hasn't happened. Sometimes simply gaining this understanding is enough to resolve an issue. Here are some examples of clarity-based requests:

- "Can you explain to me why you've shown up late every day this week?"
- "Will you help me understand why you're raising your voice?"
- "Are you willing to tell me why you didn't do what you promised you would?"

A connection-based request is the lightest touch of the three. It's useful in more complex situations or at the beginning of a longer conversation to help ease into heavier topics. Essentially, a connection-based request is used to bring awareness to someone else about your experience. Here are some examples of connection-based requests:

- "Does that make sense to you?"
- "Can you understand where I'm coming from?"
- "Can you relate to what I'm saying?"

Let's look at some examples that go through each of the steps using a different type of request.

Judy and Amanda

Judy and Amanda are college roommates, and Judy has noticed that Amanda has been drinking very heavily for the last month. Judy knows that if this behavior continues, she won't be able to live with Amanda much longer. She decides to use NVC to search for a resolution or at the very least draw a clear boundary.

JUDY

(PRECURSOR)

Hey, something has been on my mind lately,
and I was wondering if now is a good time to bring it up.

AMANDA

Sure, what's going on?

JUDY

(STEP 1)

Well, over the last few weeks I've been noticing
that you've been drinking almost every night, . . .

(STEP 2)

. . . and I'm feeling really concerned . . .

(STEP 3)

. . . because I grew up in a house with a lot of alcoholism, and since I've struggled with it myself, it's really important to me to not be around it in my home.

Now Judy can choose from three types of requests for step 4:

(STEP 4)

Would you be willing to come talk to a campus counselor with me?

(Action-based)

Or:

Would you be willing to talk about why this has been happening lately?

(Clarity-based)

Or:

Does that make sense to you?

(Connection-based)

The reality is that this is unlikely to be a very easy conversation no matter how skilled her NVC is. Most people don't want anyone poking into their personal business, especially when it involves a drinking habit. Nevertheless, Judy needs to draw some boundaries for her personal well-being, so it's a necessary conversation to have.

Given the complexity of the issue, especially with something as sensitive as alcoholism, I would generally recommend using a connection-based request to start the conversation. This will begin the process with the lightest touch, and as the conversation continues and connection builds, it will become easier to find a long-term, sustainable win-win solution.

If Judy starts off with the *action-based* request, it's unlikely to work very well because very little trust and connection have been built up yet. It would be easy for Amanda to assume that Judy is judging her and become triggered enough to lash out in anger. A *clarity-based* request has a better chance of getting good results; however, again, without enough trust and connection it can easily be brushed aside. Considering this is the beginning of what is likely to be a challenging conversation about a complex issue, I would recommend first building a sense of trust through the gentler approach of a connection-based request, allowing them to slowly ease into the conversation while minimizing the risk of Amanda taking things personally. The more Judy communicates without judgment and understands why Amanda is drinking so frequently, the better suited her eventual action-based request will likely be.

If Amanda gets triggered at any point in the conversation, Judy can switch into Emergency Empathy (covered in the next chapter) to calm her down. Once Amanda feels heard and understood from the Emergency Empathy, the connection and trust between them will be much higher than it was at the beginning of the conversation. Judy can then do another round of NVC, preferably now using a clarity-based request to gain understanding on why Amanda has been drinking so heavily.

A good general practice with complex issues is to start with a connection-based request, then go to clarity-based, and ultimately end with an action-based request. This is not a rule, but I have found it a helpful guideline. If Amanda gets triggered again at any point, then it's right back to Emergency Empathy. If she doesn't get triggered, then with this new knowledge gained from the clarity-based request, Judy can make an action-based request that will hopefully lead to a long-term, sustainable win-win solution.

Nathan and Maria

In this scenario, Nathan and Maria are a married couple who both work full-time jobs. Nathan recently received a raise but has also been working longer hours, which has led him to neglect some of his household responsibilities. Maria, feeling frustrated, decides to address the issue using NVC.

MARIA

(PRECURSOR)

Hey, babe, there's something I would like
to talk with you about. Is now a good time?

NATHAN

Sure.

MARIA

(STEP 1)

The lawn hasn't been mowed in over a month, and it's supposed to
rain tomorrow but the gutters are full of leaves.
These are both things you've agreed to stay on top of . . .

(Observable facts without judgment)

(STEP 2)

. . . and I'm feeling frustrated . . .

(Authentic feeling)

(STEP 3)

. . . because it's really important to me
for the house to be well maintained.

*(Taking responsibility for her feelings
by connecting them to her values)*

Now Maria can choose one of the following requests:

(STEP 4)

Would you be willing to take care of all those things today?

(Action-based)

Or:

Is there a reason why these haven't been taken care of?

(Clarity-based)

Or:

Do you understand where I'm coming from?

(Connection-based)

In this instance, since the issue is not overly complex, I would recommend starting with a clarity-based request. For example's sake, let's say this is an NVC household, so Nathan responds with NVC as well.

NATHAN

(STEP 1)

I totally get where you're coming from, . . .

(Internal fact)

(STEP 2)

. . . but when I think about doing all those things today,
I feel stressed out . . .

(Authentic feeling)

(STEP 3)

. . . because this is my first day off since my promotion and what I really want is to spend some quality time with you.

(Explaining his current values)

(STEP 4)

I'm thinking, since I'm making more money now, we can afford to hire some help around the house to do these chores.

I'm happy to arrange that today. Would that work for you?

(Clarity-based request)

This solution addresses both Nathan's need to relax and spend quality time with Maria and Maria's need for a well-maintained home. It offers a potential win-win solution where neither party is compromising.

Compromise

Compromise, in the modern world, is often thought of as a mature way to resolve conflict, but from an NVC perspective, it's not recommended. In a compromise, neither party gets what they truly want, even though they've come to an agreement. While this is much better than having an unresolved conflict, it's not nearly as desirable as both parties getting their full needs met. If you ever feel like you're compromising, it's usually a sign that the true root of the issue hasn't been fully uncovered. Once the real cause is brought to light, win-win solutions become much easier to find, eliminating the need for compromise.

For example, married couple Melinda and Gary can't agree on what movie to go see together. Melinda wants to see a romantic comedy, while Gary wants to see a sci-fi action film. Gary despises the actors in the romantic comedy and Melinda doesn't enjoy action movies, but neither is particularly excited about any other options available. If they compromise, they'll end up seeing a movie that at least one of them doesn't want to see. However, if they refuse to compromise and keep communicating, they may realize that the whole reason they're even going to the movies is to spend quality time together. It's not about the movie itself but rather the shared experience. Instead of going to the movies, they might decide to fulfill the underlying goal of spending quality time together by doing an activity they're both excited about, such as partner dancing, ice-skating, or going to a concert.

Not compromising doesn't mean stubbornly insisting on getting exactly what you want. It means continuing the dialogue until you find a mutually satisfying solution where nobody is compromising, even if the solution looks different from the original plan.

PREAMBLE

When you want to bring up something that has been bothering you, it can be helpful to check in with the other person before you begin speaking to see if it's a good time to talk. I have called these *precursors* in earlier dialogues, and they're usually just a line or two with no special guidelines. However, when the topic is particularly touchy or complex, using a full NVC statement, which is what I call a *preamble*, can be extremely helpful. This sets the stage for a more receptive and productive conversation. Here are a couple of examples:

(STEP 1)

Hey, there's something that's been bothering me, . . .

(STEP 2)

. . . and I'm feeling a bit concerned . . .

(STEP 3)

. . . that if we don't talk about it, it could become an issue,
and I really want to maintain a strong
and healthy relationship with you.

(STEP 4)

Is now a good time to talk?

(STEP 1)

Hi, honey, I've noticed myself feeling a little anxious every time I think about something that happened last week, . . .

(STEP 2)

. . . and I'm worried . . .

(STEP 3)

. . . that if I don't bring it up, it will create issues down the line.

(STEP 4)

So I was wondering if we can sit and talk about it sometime today.

These statements achieve several important things at once. First, they acknowledge that the other person's time and emotional state are valuable. This will immediately help put the other person at ease because even a well-structured NVC statement is unlikely to be effective if the other person isn't emotionally prepared to give you their undivided attention. Second, these statements communicate that the relationship is important and you want to be proactive about keeping it healthy. This helps create an environment that's more conducive to solving conflicts and building connection instead of being defensive.

After the preamble, if they agree, you can discuss the actual issue that is bothering you. While this isn't a strict rule, it's a good practice to at least check if it's a good time to talk before getting into a deeper conversation. If it's not a good time, then as long as you are dealing with a reasonable person, it should be relatively easy to schedule it for another time that works for both of you. If for some reason they refuse to schedule a time to talk at all, unless there are legitimate logistical reasons, this suggests there are serious underlying issues that probably need to be addressed first. No relationship can survive and thrive without communication.

These four steps form a basic understanding of the key elements of NVC. It's incredibly useful for drawing boundaries, resolving conflicts, and addressing sensitive issues. For further study, I highly recommend reading Marshall Rosenberg's book *Nonviolent Communication*, as well as my book, *The Art of Nonviolent Communication.* Listening to NVC-focused podcasts, including mine, *The Art of NVC*, can also provide valuable insights.

5

Emergency Empathy

EMERGENCY EMPATHY is the element that transforms NVC from a theoretical concept into a powerful, practical tool that can be used in real-world interactions. When people are triggered and flooded with intense emotions, they can easily become belligerent and overpower even the most skillful NVC attempts. Emergency Empathy bridges this gap, allowing NVC to remain effective even in the heat of the most emotionally charged moments.

Humans are emotional beings, and emotions are both powerful and unpredictable. They don't need to follow logical or linear paths and at times arise with such intensity that conversations can rapidly spiral out of control. This emotional volatility is what often turns simple misunderstandings into heated conflicts, even with well-done NVC. Thankfully, this is where Emergency Empathy comes in. It has the power to rapidly rebuild connection with someone who is triggered and allow for productive conversation to continue. It will work in moments when almost nothing else will. No matter how skilled and gentle your NVC is, rest assured, there will come a moment when you need to use Emergency Empathy.

WHAT IS EMERGENCY EMPATHY?

Emergency Empathy involves two steps: guessing how someone feels and guessing why they feel that way. It's truly that simple. Yet if you've ever tried it, you know that simple does not always mean easy. This technique is primarily used to maintain or establish connection and de-escalate intense interactions. The biggest challenge lies in the fact that Emergency Empathy is needed most during moments when it feels hardest to implement. In those moments, it will often feel like the last thing you want to do, even though it may be the only thing that will work. A bit of a conundrum, to say the least.

The difficulty comes from the nature of dealing with someone who is deeply triggered. When people are in this state, their pain body takes control, and they often:

- Lie
- Exaggerate
- Guilt-trip
- Distort the truth
- Threaten
- Insult
- Yell
- Cry
- Take things out of context
- Lash out in hurtful ways
- Use straw man tactics
- Bring up unrelated things from the past that portray you unfavorably

A triggered person will often use any tactic possible to attack and discredit you. This is a reality of human interaction. When attacked like this, some common responses might include:

- Defending yourself
- Correcting the lies and exaggerations with facts
- Repeating your points
- Trying to reason with them using logic
- Attacking back
- Shutting down and avoiding

The problem is that none of these strategies will help reach a win-win solution. Instead, they will often escalate the situation further. This is because when someone is triggered, their body reacts as if they are in a life-or-death situation. Adrenaline is pumping through their veins, and their cerebral cortex (responsible for logic and reason) is temporarily shut down. In this state they're not looking for a win-win solution; they're looking to win right now at all costs. Logic and facts have no hope of changing their mind in such moments.

Thankfully there's Emergency Empathy, which has the power to pierce through even the most intensely triggered brain in mere moments. Here's why: Emergency Empathy is about asking two very specific questions about the other person's internal world, an uncommon and surprising experience for many people. Your interest in their emotional state—a topic they are an expert in—shows them that you care about their well-being and who they are as a person, a tactic that can calm their overactive nervous system and help them feel safe. Regardless of a person's self-image, most people want to be seen and heard, and showing them that you're willing to do so is a powerful thing. These factors all work together to make it almost impossible to ignore a properly phrased Emergency Empathy question, no matter how upset someone is in that moment.

Well-meaning people who genuinely want to help often ask questions like "Are you upset?" or "What's wrong?" While these come from a caring place, they don't work very well by themselves.

They're too open-ended; they lack vulnerability and leave too much work for the other person. Thus they can easily be ignored or deflected. Emergency Empathy, on the other hand, is a one-two punch. You need to use both the *feeling* and *why* they might feel that way for it to work. There's a big difference between asking, "Are you upset?" and asking, "Are you upset because you would like more appreciation for all the work you've been doing around the house?" The first one can easily be denied or ignored with little thought. The second one is so detailed and specific that it will prompt a much more thorough response. When you take the time and energy to suggest a possible reason for their discomfort, it shows you care. It feels good to be asked about our internal life when there's no judgment attached. In my opinion, it feels like being loved.

Here are some more examples of these one-two-punch questions.

HELPFUL: "Are you feeling stressed because you think it will make a bad impression if we show up ten minutes late?"
UNHELPFUL: "Are you stressed right now?"
VERY UNHELPFUL: "Why are you so stressed right now?" (This is worse because it implies they shouldn't be feeling stressed.)

HELPFUL: "Are you feeling sad because you wanted to spend more alone time together?"
UNHELPFUL: "What's wrong?"
VERY UNHELPFUL: "Why are you so sad?"

I have to regularly remind my students that it takes both parts of the question—identifying both the feeling and why they're feeling it—for it to be considered Emergency Empathy. I believe their reluctance comes from the emotional work it takes to ask someone something so personal. It requires genuine thought and focus. There's risk involved because you might be totally wrong. It's much easier to just ask how they feel, but it will never be as effective in building connection and uncovering the heart of the matter.

Every time someone responds to your questions, whether you've correctly identified their feelings or not, the situation will get at least a little bit calmer, and you will have at least a little more information to work with. This is progress toward a win-win solution and should be acknowledged, especially when you consider how quickly arguments can spiral out of control.

While identifying our feelings is often straightforward, *why* we feel that way may require some introspection. It's not uncommon for someone to be sure they're upset but not entirely sure about the cause. When you frame the Emergency Empathy questions correctly, they're so compelling that the person will be forced to focus internally to respond, even if only for a moment. Focusing attention internally has a calming effect. This is why it's the fundamental principle in many meditation techniques. When we're projecting our attention on the outside world and the grievances we have, it often brings up negative feelings including agitation, anger, fear, and helplessness. When we focus on our interior world, everything slows down a bit and a sense of peace begins to emanate from us. There's less to distract or agitate us, creating a natural calm. Even brief moments of this internal focus can have a noticeable effect. This is one of several reasons why each round of Emergency Empathy tends to create a progressively more relaxed and grounded atmosphere.

EMERGENCY EMPATHY CHALLENGES

The first step to successfully employing Emergency Empathy is to ask the person who is triggered if they're feeling a specific feeling. This may sound simple, yet there are a variety of challenges that will make it far more difficult than it may seem at first. We have already covered the difference between a real feeling and a faux feeling in chapter 3, but it is relevant here as well. For example, let's look at this question: "Are you feeling mistreated because I used swear words in your presence?" The problem with this statement is it's unclear whether you are admitting fault or not. It could easily be interpreted that you are implying you mistreated them, you are wrong and bad for doing that, you're responsible for their distress, and this might be an attempt at an apology. Emergency Empathy is not about admitting fault and apologizing. Instead, it's a neutral attempt at identifying how someone feels and why. Nothing more, nothing less. It doesn't mean you are agreeing, condoning, or condemning any behavior. You just want to uncover how they currently feel and why. If you want to apologize, it's much better to say something along the lines of "You're right, and I'm sorry." The less room for confusion and misinterpretation the better.

Remember, as discussed in previous chapters, we are all responsible for how we feel at all times because our feelings depend on how we are framing the situation in our own minds. When you use faux feelings in an Emergency Empathy statement, it implies you are responsible for how the other person feels. This is inaccurate and to be avoided because of the confusion it brings. Now, to be clear, despite incorrectly using a faux feeling, this can at times get decent results. Doing Emergency Empathy incorrectly is still far better than most reactions. However, I highly recommend striving to remove faux feelings from your NVC altogether, and I can assure you that your results will vastly improve.

Here is a correctly phrased alternative Emergency Empathy question from the same circumstances: "Are you feeling upset because you don't like when people use swear words in your presence?" This is a neutral attempt at understanding without assigning blame in any direction and acknowledges that the other person's feelings would be a result of their own preferences being met or not. Some people really dislike swear words; others don't mind them at all. It doesn't inherently mean you are mistreating someone by swearing around them unless they have clearly stated they would prefer you not to, which is something that can be uncovered if this conversation were to continue.

The next major challenge is to dodge every insult and resist every urge to correct, defend, or condemn the attacks of the person who is triggered. Instead, you must turn into a neutral detective as you take a stab in the dark and guess how they feel and why. This can be a very difficult and awkward feeling, but it's absolutely necessary. If you don't, you risk becoming triggered yourself from one of the many violent tactics being used against you, and any chance of a sustainable, long-term win-win solution will become much harder. This doesn't mean you need to be a punching bag. Once the situation calms down, you can address every single issue that is bothering you, including how they just acted when they were triggered. While you're doing Emergency Empathy, though, you must take nothing personally and instead focus on identifying how they feel and why. Remind yourself that you are not agreeing or disagreeing, neither are you condoning or condemning. You are simply identifying. A deep breath can help in these moments, as well as remembering that they are probably in their pain body and feeling a rush of intense emotion. Therefore, their words are harsher than they would normally be. Most of us have likely acted in similar ways at times. Provide them with the grace you would like if the situation were reversed and continue on with the goal of uncovering how they feel and why.

Of course there are limits to what is acceptable to say and do. And if you are ever in fear for your own safety, it's probably better to do what it takes to feel safe before attempting anything else.

It's Okay to Be Wrong

A key preliminary understanding is that you do not have to be correct. You're going to be wrong many times. This is important to embrace fully. You'll be wrong, and *that's okay*. It's normal. There is no realistic way to always be correct at guessing what's going on with someone else's complex inner world. You're simply beginning a process, and it will likely take a few rounds of guessing as you home in on the truth. The important thing is to use the proper techniques, which means using real feelings and avoiding all implications of wrongdoing or judgments.

Every time you guess how someone feels and why, even if you're wrong, there will still be a benefit because, if you pay close attention, they'll give you clues about their true feelings and reasons why they feel that way. In these moments, it's good to remember that people rarely speak directly, so you have to listen to the subtext. Be a neutral detective. They'll probably beat around the bush a bit before giving you an honest and direct answer. That's okay. Listen precisely to how they phrase their responses.

What did they not say? Why did they word it like that? What would you mean if you said that? Take this information and use it in your next round of Emergency Empathy.

Going Deeper

When practicing Emergency Empathy, you want to continually go deeper as opposed to staying with surface-level questions. Shallow questions are much easier to ask, but they're also much easier to deflect or ignore. Deeper questions take more energy and courage and also tend to produce responses that are more vulnerable and meaningful.

If someone gets intensely triggered by something as small as a toothpaste cap left off the tube, it's likely the cap is not the real issue. It's the surface-level concern masking a deeper, more important feeling or need. For example: David sees that his college-age son Casper left the cap off the toothpaste again, and he speaks to him in an exasperated tone:

DAVID

Why's it so hard for you to simply do
even the smallest things I ask of you?

Is David really mad about the toothpaste, or is he upset about what he thinks this means in some broader context? If Casper was to do Emergency Empathy on the most surface level, it might sound something like this:

CASPER

Are you feeling upset because I left the cap off again?

While this response is better than reacting with anger, insults, or defensiveness, it doesn't dig into the real issue. It simply echoes what David has already said, without creating any new understanding or connection. If I was coaching Casper, I'd advise him to:

1. **TAKE A DEEP BREATH** and ignore any impulse to respond with anger, defend, or attack back.
2. **ASSUME THE TOOTHPASTE ISN'T THE REAL ISSUE** and it's up to him to use Emergency Empathy to find out the deeper, underlying concern—because if he doesn't, who will? Most likely not his father, who is already showing signs of being triggered.
3. **BE SPECIFIC,** and even if his first guess is wrong, listen closely to the response from his dad and try again until his dad feels calm and there's a sense of connection between them.

I'd also warn him that this process might feel awkward, especially if this is the beginning of his NVC journey, but that's completely normal. Here is how Casper might follow this advice:

CASPER

Are you feeling upset because you think
I'm purposely leaving the cap off just to annoy you?

Is this the most brilliant and perceptive Emergency Empathy possible? No, but it also doesn't have to be. In the heat of the moment, time is limited. It's more important to express something that follows the fundamental principles of NVC, even if it's basic, rather than hesitating while searching for something brilliant. And even if this isn't the true reason David is upset, it will still de-escalate the interaction and build a bit of connection. Remember, people appreciate being seen and asked about their inner world, even if your observation isn't 100 percent correct. In moments like these, every little bit helps.

After hearing Casper's question, David is likely to clarify whether or not his emotional assessment was correct.

DAVID

I just don't understand how you're ever gonna graduate law school
if you can't even put the cap back on the toothpaste.

At this point, Casper must once again resist any urge to defend himself, use sarcasm, make judgments, insult, or point out flaws in David's statement. Instead, he should engage in another round of Emergency Empathy, going deeper based on David's response.

CASPER

Are you feeling worried because this is the first time
I'll be away from home for so long and law school
is such a stressful environment?

David must think about this for a moment. As he does, he calms down a bit more and speaks in a gentler tone.

DAVID

I just want you to have the best chance at succeeding,
and when I see things like this, I get worried about you.

Now that David has calmed down and there is a mutual feeling of connection between them, Casper can address the toothpaste issue directly, because David is much more likely to listen now that his concerns have been acknowledged and understood.

CASPER

Okay, I can see how that could be a little concerning.
In light of that, I promise to do my best to put the cap
back on the toothpaste every time. It's the least I can do,
since you're paying for my really expensive college.

They both laugh and move into a heartfelt conversation addressing the challenges Casper is likely to face at school. Had Casper started with a defensive response instead of Emergency Empathy, it's unlikely the conversation would have gone so well. In fact, it could have gone horribly wrong because David was still triggered and until he calmed down, he would have been difficult to reason with. That's why it's always *Emergency Empathy first*, followed by facts and logic once emotions have settled.

6

Building on the Essential Principles

There are only a few essential principles to make sure you follow at all times when practicing NVC, which include:

- Being nonjudgmental
- Avoiding any implication that anyone is bad or wrong
- Being authentic and honest

These principles are absolutely crucial. I recommend striving to follow them at all times without exception while doing NVC or Emergency Empathy. Even if this is all you do, your communication skills will drastically improve. However, not every principle has to be followed so rigidly. In this chapter I will break down several principles that are highly beneficial but are okay to bend here and there, depending on the circumstances, especially if they help you sound natural. In my opinion, sounding natural is far more important than perfect technique. If you come across as if you're "doing something" instead of speaking from the heart in your natural voice, it will be far less effective, and your conversation partner will likely be on guard against you, making connection more difficult.

HOW TO SOUND NATURAL

One way to sound natural is to avoid using obscure words that aren't a part of your normal vocabulary. Feelings such as *mortified* or *chagrined* are valid feelings but these words will probably not sound natural to the majority of people today (unless you frequently use those words in your everyday conversations). In most cases, you can go a long way with more common feeling words such as *concerned*, *upset*, *frustrated*, *annoyed*, *worried*, *stressed*, *sad*, or *overwhelmed*.

Another way to sound natural is through the phrasing you choose. There are some common NVC phrases that I personally avoid using because they're always a dead giveaway that NVC is being used. For example, which of these sounds more natural?

"Are you upset because it's hard for you to relax unless the house is clean?"

"Do you feel chagrined because you have a need for a clean house?"

The answer is subjective depending on how you normally speak, but to me the first one sounds far more natural than the second, both in phrasing and choice of words. If someone said the second example to me, all kinds of alarm bells would go off in my head, telling me something weird was happening, and I would be on guard. This doesn't mean the interaction is destined to go wrong if you sound awkward or someone knows you're using NVC. Rather, it might be a little harder to get them to open up and be vulnerable with you, which is usually where the magic is.

In his original book on NVC, Marshall Rosenberg often uses

the concept of *needs*, asking questions such as "Do you have a need for more appreciation?" or "Do you have a need for more privacy?" I prefer not to use the word *need* because it sounds a bit extreme in my opinion, as if it implies a life-or-death situation. Also, it's not language I would normally use outside of NVC. Instead of saying, "Are you feeling upset because you have a need for a clean kitchen?" I would say something like, "Are you feeling upset because . . .

- . . . a clean kitchen is important to you?"
- . . . you value cleanliness?"
- . . . you prefer the kitchen to be cleaner than it is right now?"
- . . . you don't like when the kitchen is in this state?"

To me, all of these sound more natural and will have a far greater chance at getting a genuine response—even the last example, which phrases it in the negative with a "you don't like" statement. In his book, Rosenberg specifies that people are more likely to respond favorably if you state things in a way that highlights what *you do* want instead of what *you don't* want, and I agree. Ideally it's better to phrase things in the positive, but most important is what works. If phrasing something in the negative sounds more natural to you and gets the point across, then I'm okay with my students doing this. Is it perfect technique? Probably not by most NVC teachers' standards, but this is an art form, not a rigid rule-based system. The goal is to build connection, draw boundaries, and find long-term win-win solutions to conflicts, not perfection.

ASKING VERSUS TELLING

One of the reasons Emergency Empathy is so effective at piercing the defenses of a triggered mind is it allows the other person to be the expert in how they feel. This is done by *asking* and not *telling* them. There's a significant difference between "Are you feeling frustrated because you would like more help around the house?" and "Clearly you're frustrated because you want more help around the house." When you *tell* someone how they feel, you're essentially assuming the role of the expert on their emotions. The issue with this approach is that you can never truly know someone's internal experience better than they do.

By asking, you allow the other person to remain the expert, which encourages them to share valuable insights and details that will help you get to the root of the issue. If you tell them how they feel, you're more likely to encounter resistance, even if you're accurate. Asking almost forces them to put their attention on their internal world, which, as we've seen in the examples, creates a calming effect. The act of asking a question is also more vulnerable than telling: When you ask, you're acknowledging you may be incorrect. Telling, on the other hand, presents your statement as a fact, implying that any discussion or debate is irrelevant. Remember, *asking* creates space for dialogue, while *telling* stifles it.

AVOID OBVIOUS PATTERNS

People are highly sensitive to patterns, and if they detect one in your speech, it can again signal to them that you're "doing something" instead of being your natural self. Here are a few examples of patterns you might experience while starting out.

Repeated Feelings

When using Emergency Empathy, it often takes more than one round of guessing to accurately identify the other person's feelings and reasons. With that in mind, it's crucial to vary the feeling you guess each time, as repeating the same feeling over and over can easily derail the entire conversation. Imagine if someone asked you the following questions in a row:

- "Are you feeling annoyed because you would like more quiet?"
- "Are you feeling annoyed because you want to be alone?"
- "Are you feeling annoyed because you're having trouble with what you are working on?"
- "Are you feeling annoyed because you might not meet your deadline?"

If you weren't annoyed at the start of these questions, you probably would be by the end, because essentially you're being told you're annoyed, just in a roundabout way.

It's much better to change the feeling each time instead of repeating the same one over and over. If you think the first feeling was correct, but you're still guessing why they feel that way, you can interchange it with similar feelings such *frustrated*, *stressed*, *concerned*, or *upset*. For example:

- "Are you feeling annoyed because you would like more quiet?"
- "Are you feeling frustrated because you want to be alone?"
- "Are you feeling upset because you're having trouble with what you are working on?"
- "Are you feeling worried because you might not meet your deadline?"

When dealing with triggered individuals, small adjustments like these can make a huge difference.

So which feelings should you use? Despite the complexity of our inner lives, there really isn't a huge variety of feelings that we need to memorize. I rarely find myself using anything beyond these twelve:

- Concerned
- Upset
- Annoyed
- Frustrated
- Worried
- Stressed
- Anxious
- Lonely
- Sad
- Scared
- Angry
- Overwhelmed

I recommend having at least ten or twelve emotions that you like to use in your repertoire, and I wouldn't worry about it too much after that. You don't need pinpoint emotional accuracy for Emergency Empathy to be effective. Often just getting in the emotional ballpark is enough for them to open up.

Reiterated Phrasing

The second pattern I would advise to be aware of is how you phrase your guesses. Repeating the same phrasing will eventually stand out and alert the person that you're following a formula, which could also derail any progress you've made. I recommend never using the same phrasing more than twice in a row. Here is a scenario to help illustrate this point.

Christie and Candice are roommates in college. Christie is in the dining room studying, and Candice comes into the kitchen to get something to eat but notices the fridge door is open. She instantly becomes triggered and speaks in an aggressive tone:

CANDICE

Is it really so hard to just shut the door
before you walk off and stuff your face?

Christie immediately feels hurt and triggered and instinctively wants to fire back, but she pauses, takes a deep breath, and chooses to use Emergency Empathy instead.

CHRISTIE

Are you feeling upset because you think
that some of your food might have gotten spoiled?

Candice responds in a slightly more calm but still aggressive tone:

CANDICE

Well, it will if this keeps happening! I'm not made of money!
Not everybody's parents are rich!

Again, I want to point out that Christie's first attempt was not a brilliantly perceptive guess that solved everything in an instant. Though this may happen on occasion, it's not something to expect every time. What's important is that she guessed about Candice's internal world without any judgments or implications of wrongdoing. Nearly anything else she could have said would have likely escalated the encounter into a full-blown argument. Instead, Candice got a little more calm and offered some clues as to what the true underlying issue is. Christie can now refine her next guess:

CHRISTIE

Are you feeling annoyed because you think that if
I keep doing things like leaving the fridge open,
our electric bill is going to be really high this month?

CANDICE

Money is tight right now! Okay?

Once again, Candice responded in a slightly calmer tone, though still a bit aggressive, so Christie proceeds to do another round of Emergency Empathy. However, here is where I want Christie to change the pattern. If she does another round of Emergency Empathy in the same format of "Are you feeling . . . because of . . .," Candice will probably subconsciously or consciously notice the pattern, which can derail the positive momentum that is going on. Instead of repeating that phrasing, she could try:

- "Is the main thing bothering you . . ."
- "Is the core issue right now . . ."
- "Is what's really getting under your skin the fact that . . ."

These replace the specific feeling question with a general acknowledgment that a negative emotion is occurring and thus completely change the pattern while still sticking to the underlying principles of addressing the feeling and why they feel that way. For example:

CHRISTIE

Is the main issue the fact that you're worried
about paying the bills this month because of
some unexpected expenses you had?

Candice responds in an almost normal tone of voice:

CANDICE

I didn't have any unexpected expenses.
Just a lot of expected ones.

Now Christie can go back to the earlier phrasing.

CHRISTIE

Are you stressed because something happened at work?

CANDICE

Actually, yeah. Look, I'm sorry I'm being so rude.
I'm just so stressed out. I got let go yesterday
and I don't know what I'm gonna do.

Candice breaks down in tears. Christie consoles her, and they are back to having a heartfelt conversation without worrying about using proper NVC and Emergency Empathy. The connection level is high, their friendship is intact, and they can work together on finding a solution rather than getting caught in a drawn-out argument.

With every round of Emergency Empathy, Candice got more and more calm. Christie kept listening to her responses and went deeper with her guesses until she found out the true underlying issue. Once she discovered Candice had lost her job, everything made sense, and it was obvious that she didn't need to keep doing more rounds of Emergency Empathy. If Christie had continued to use the exact same phrasing with every question, the conversation could have gone very differently and been much less well received.

The key understanding here is this: Patterns are to be avoided or at least disguised when possible. Do not repeat feelings back-to-back and do not use similar phrasing more than two times in a row. This will help you sound natural and avoid getting responses like,

- "Why are you talking so weird right now?"
- "Are you doing NVC again?"
- "You sound like a therapist or something."
- "Can you just talk normal to me please?"

Sometimes, even if you are being careful to avoid patterns, the other person may still recognize that you're using these tools and have this response, especially if they are someone you have a significant relationship with. This feedback can be very challenging to overcome in the moment. Here are some responses to help if this comes up:

- "Yes, I'm doing NVC because this relationship is important to me and I think that it will really help in the long run."
- "Yes, I'm doing NVC, and I apologize if it's a bit clunky right now, but I think it can really help us have a stronger relationship."
- "Yes, I've been learning NVC because I want to go the extra mile to make sure I have tools to help in the challenging moments of this and all my relationships."

This all may seem like a lot of work to do on a moment's notice, but what are the alternatives? Having a huge fight? Staying quiet to avoid conflict and building up resentment that ultimately leads to disconnection? Avoiding ever getting close to people? NVC and Emergency Empathy can be challenging, but they're by far the best tools that I've ever come across for building strong, connected, and durable relationships. The work is well worth the payoff!

7

Working with Ego

EGOS ARE OFTEN the biggest obstacle when attempting to use Emergency Empathy, and not just the ego of the other person. Our own ego is what pushes us to defend ourselves, strike back, or try to "win" the conversation. This is one of the least effective strategies for building connection or finding lasting solutions. Without a solid awareness of our own ego and the tricks it likes to play, our ability to do NVC and Emergency Empathy in intense interactions will be severely limited.

As with many words, *ego* can have multiple definitions. In the context of this book, I am using *ego* to refer to a person's self-identity. How you see yourself and how you want others to see you can be considered your ego. Many people use the concept of having a big ego as a negative trait. I believe it's a bit more nuanced.

The issue isn't with thinking of yourself as a strong, intelligent, good-looking, capable person with high integrity (what some might call a "big ego"). In fact, developing a strong self-identity is often needed to take the risks necessary to achieve success. The challenges arise when you become *attached* to that identity. For example, if John considers himself to be highly skilled at golf based on his training regimen and past successes, this can be considered perfectly normal. However, if he loses his temper every time he performs poorly or is outplayed, this signals an unhealthy attachment to his ego.

When someone you're talking with is triggered and starts hurling insults, spreading lies, or exaggerating every flaw or slight misstep you've ever made, it's your ego that will be taking the hits, and it's your ego that will want to fight back. This impulse, however, is the exact opposite of what it takes to be effective at Emergency Empathy. Instead of defending or retaliating, you must dodge the verbal attacks and focus solely on responding with Emergency Empathy. Later, when things have calmed down, you can address the attacks if desired.

In the moment, you need to act both like a martial artist, gracefully avoiding each blow, and a "Marshall" artist (after the creator of NVC, Marshall Rosenberg), responding only with empathy. You'll need to take nothing personally. But the problem is that your ego wants to take everything personally. It will scream about the injustice of the situation, telling you Emergency Empathy doesn't work, it's a silly waste of time, and you should put this person in their place immediately. Your ability to remain calm and unfazed in these moments will be dependent on how attached you are to your ego.

For example, if someone accuses you of lying, but you pride yourself on being honest, your ego will likely want to correct them and point out *their* lies. Yet what will it help? Do you think the triggered person will hear your accusations and instantly calm down and apologize? Highly unlikely. What's *more* likely to happen is that they will ignore or deflect your comments and launch a new attack. Now your ego will insist on defending itself again, but this time with even more vigor, and soon you will be in a full-blown argument—exactly what this book is designed to help you avoid.

Instead, what I'm asking you to do, to the deep chagrin of egos everywhere, is to ignore their attacks and try to imagine how this other person feels right then and why they might feel that way. Your ego will shout, *How am I supposed to know how they feel and why? They're so unreasonable it could be anything!* And it isn't necessarily wrong. It can be challenging to immediately pinpoint someone else's precise feeling and reason behind it in the heat of the moment. This is why you have to *guess* and be perfectly willing to be *wrong*. Another of our ego's least favorite activities.

The strategy I recommend is to momentarily put yourself in their shoes. Imagine you are them and ask yourself, *If I was saying the things they're saying to me, how would I be feeling? Why might I feel this way?* This takes effort and focus, especially since you're under fire. It can help if you think of yourself as a neutral detective on a case. Your whole job is to identify how they feel and why. You're not agreeing or disagreeing with them, nor are you condoning or condemning their behavior. You're simply identifying. This process may feel like a mini death to your ego, and in a way it is. You're releasing your identity for a moment in order to fully embody someone else's perspective. Your normal self disappears along with all its concerns, and now you're a neutral detective on a case.

Once you commit to this, their insults become meaningless and effortless to avoid. It's not even the current *you* they're talking about. You're someone on a mission, and as soon as you get an insight, you'll do another round of Emergency Empathy, perfectly willing to be wrong and listening closely to exactly how they respond to refine your next attempt. Once the feeling and its source are identified, a magical thing happens: The person who was triggered calms down. They now realize they've been heard and understood. Their ego exhales. There's no more reason for them to shout, defend, or prove anything. Now they have open ears to hear you and the conversation can continue in a normal tone.

You cannot simultaneously cater to the whims of your ego and effectively do Emergency Empathy. It's one or the other. Your ego knows this and will use every trick in the book to keep you from abandoning it. In the beginning, I often had to mentally yell, *Do Emergency Empathy! Do Emergency Empathy! Do Emergency Empathy!* to drown out my ego's protests and commit to it. It can feel awkward at first—that is, until it starts working. When the other person calms down and an argument is avoided, it starts to feel like a superpower.

Let's use an example to illustrate these concepts. Janet, a single mom working from home, is under immense pressure. She has a major project due in the morning that could be pivotal for her career, and it requires all of her focus and expertise. After several days of little sleep and long hours, she finally sits down for the homestretch. But just as she begins, she hears loud music blasting from her fifteen-year-old daughter Vanessa's room, so loud that it rattles the pictures on her walls.

Janet feels her stress levels spike. Vanessa knows about the deadline, and even if she didn't, the music is way too loud! Janet storms to Vanessa's room furious, but halfway there she stops. She makes a conscious decision: Instead of reacting in anger, she will use NVC. She takes a deep breath and knocks on Vanessa's door. After no response, she enters the room and finds Vanessa on her bed scrolling through her phone, music blaring.

JANET

Honey, can I talk with you about something?

Vanessa rolls her eyes and reluctantly turns down the music. Janet ignores the rolled eyes for the moment and begins a proper NVC statement that will end in her specific request.

JANET

(STEP 1)

The music you're playing is rattling the pictures on my walls.

(STEP 2)

I'm feeling very stressed . . .

(STEP 3)

. . . because I have a huge deadline to finish tonight, but it's really hard for me to focus with the music so loud.

(STEP 4)

Would you be willing to turn down your music or use headphones so that I won't hear it from my room?

This is correctly done NVC. It sounds natural, contains only facts, and is void of all judgments. Janet feels happy she avoided using any of her normal violent language and still expressed herself authentically. Unfortunately, Vanessa doesn't share her sentiment and responds in an aggressive, disdainful tone only a teenager can use:

VANESSA

Oh my gosh, Mom, why are you being such a princess? If a little bit of music stops you from getting your work done, I don't know how you're managing in the real world. Leave me alone and grow up!

Janet is stunned at the sheer audacity of what her teenage daughter just said to her. She can barely believe her fifteen-year-old told her to grow up. Here Janet is, doing her best to be polite and respectful, while her daughter couldn't care less.

Janet's ego flares up. She wants to tell Vanessa that she has no idea what she's talking about, demand respect, and threaten to take her phone away. Her ego also wants to list all her professional achievements and everything her hard work has provided for Vanessa. But instead of letting her ego take over, Janet chooses to respond with Emergency Empathy. Unfortunately, before she can get a word out, her ego fights back, saying, *This is a waste of time! How are we supposed to know how she feels and why? She's a teenager with raging hormones! You have work to finish!* But Janet takes a deep breath while yelling in her own head, *Do Emergency Empathy! Do Emergency Empathy!* This helps her shake off her ego's attempts to sabotage the interaction, and she recommits to doing Emergency Empathy.

However, she suddenly feels nervous and awkward. She's finding it hard to think of anything brilliant, so she says the first thing that comes to mind, knowing it needs to be free of judgment and focused on a real feeling.

JANET

Are you upset because you don't think I love you?

Janet's ego immediately says, *That was the dumbest thing you could have said! You look silly!* Janet does feel silly, but to her surprise, Vanessa responds in a slightly less aggressive tone.

VANESSA

What? No. I'm not upset because I think you don't love me. I know you love me. And anyway, I'm not upset. My life is perfect. Everything is perfect!

Vanessa says this as a tear rolls down her face, which she angrily wipes away.

VANESSA

Ignore that!

JANET

Are you feeling sad about losing the volleyball game today?

Vanessa replies in a slightly calmer tone.

VANESSA

No, I don't even care about volleyball.

Janet remembers she has to change the pattern since she's just used the same phrasing twice.

JANET

Does the main thing that's bothering you have anything to do with your boyfriend, Jesse?

VANESSA

He's not my boyfriend anymore! We broke up!

Vanessa breaks down crying. Janet goes over and gives her a hug, no longer upset about the loud music. They end up talking for a heartfelt fifteen minutes, sharing a much needed mother-daughter bonding session. Vanessa thanks her for the talk and apologizes for playing the music so loud as she puts on headphones. Janet is able to go back to work feeling a deeper sense of connection with her daughter.

This is the kind of result you can get when using Emergency Empathy and NVC correctly. With proper technique, you will be able to avoid fights and build connection at the same time as resolving issues. Yes, your ego will fight you, especially in the beginning, but eventually it will get easier as long as you commit and follow the fundamental principles.

In this chapter we've seen a few examples of how to deal with your ego before it gets too in the way: repeating a phrase, pretending you're a neutral detective, and taking deep breaths. These are all things that have helped me and many of my students, but they certainly aren't the only methods that will work. In the end, there is no cookie-cutter solution to dealing with ego, so you may have to do some investigative work on your own to figure out what works best for you.

8

Weaving Together NVC and Emergency Empathy

CONFLICTS CAN ARISE in countless ways. Sometimes they appear in the heat of the moment, catching you off guard, while other times they slowly build over weeks or even years. They can often emerge when discussing a sensitive topic or attempting to set a boundary. No matter how it appears, you always have the choice of beginning with Emergency Empathy or Nonviolent Communication. In most cases, you'll be switching back and forth between them, depending on your preference and what the intensity level of the conversation demands.

Though Emergency Empathy is specifically designed to de-escalate heightened emotions when someone is triggered, it can also be used to simply build connection or break the ice anytime you choose. I often employ an "empathy first" strategy, which means as soon as I sense even the slightest hint of an issue, I immediately go into Emergency Empathy to steer things in a positive and connected direction. Sometimes this alone is enough to solve conflicts before they even start.

NVC, on the other hand, is only to be used when people are still relatively calm, and this is a definite rule. Trying to use NVC with someone who is triggered is ineffective and can be extremely frustrating for both parties. Triggered people are not open to logic, facts, or reason. If your goal is to reach a resolution efficiently, using NVC while they're in that state is counterproductive. Once a triggered person understands they've been heard and understood from Emergency Empathy, you can resume doing NVC until a win-win solution is found. If they become triggered again, you must instantly switch back into Emergency Empathy. You'll know you're done doing Emergency Empathy by the feeling in the room between you and whoever you are in a conflict with. The energy or feeling in the room is far more important than the words being exchanged.

Sometimes you may do a round of Emergency Empathy and the person might say, "Yes, that's exactly how I feel," but the energy in the room doesn't change. If there's still tension in the air, you can rest assured something deeper is going on that has yet to be identified, signaling it's time for another round of Emergency Empathy. On other occasions, you may deliver a surprisingly accurate round of Emergency Empathy that penetrates the other person's heart. They might instantly break down in tears and the animosity in the room evaporates, as we saw in the last chapter with Janet and Vanessa. Hearing someone else describe your feelings and the reasons behind them has a unique power to do this. When this occurs, you will know you've broken through and a resolution is near.

Some issues can be resolved in a single conversation, while others will require multiple discussions. This is important to remember so you can have realistic expectations. Complex issues, especially those rooted in long-term relationships—infidelity, addiction, or health challenges, for example—may take time to fully resolve, and that's okay. For resolving a deep-seated issue, all that's truly needed is a *potential* win-win solution. This is a step in the right direction, and that's a powerful thing. A potential solution may or may not work out, but it doesn't have to. If it works out, that's wonderful. If it doesn't, then you now have more information about the nature of the issue and what it will take to fully resolve it. You can use this information for the next potential solution until you've uncovered a genuine, sustainable win-win resolution. By using a mixture of NVC and Emergency Empathy, you will be able to navigate through conflicts of any level of complexity.

Let's use an example to illustrate these ideas. Mark and Jack are brothers in their thirties. Mark is getting married in six months, and due to Jack's history with alcohol, Mark has chosen not to invite Jack to the wedding if he plans to drink. Mark knows this will be a tough conversation, so he invites Jack out to lunch and lets him know there's something important they need to talk about.

Jack arrives a few minutes late looking stressed, so Mark decides to use the "empathy first" strategy and opens with the first thing that pops into his mind:

MARK

Are you feeling stressed because you think
I'm gonna tell you I have cancer or something?

JACK

The thought did cross my mind.

MARK

No, it's nothing like that.

JACK

Okay, glad to hear that. But I don't have a lot of time
so let's just get right into it, if you don't mind.

MARK

No problem.

Things are calm enough, so Mark goes into NVC to let him know what his concerns are.

MARK

(STEP 1)

As you know, Kate and I are getting married in August, and we're putting together the final guest list, . . .

(STEP 2)

. . . and I'm feeling nervous about inviting you, . . .

(STEP 3)

. . . because there'll be an open bar at the wedding and it's important to me that the day goes off without any drama.

(STEP 4)

Do you understand where I'm coming from?

Despite Mark's well-delivered NVC, Jack's response is defensive and emotionally charged.

JACK

What are you talking about? What I don't understand is why you're gonna let some chick get between you and your family. It's pathetic, if you ask me.

Mark instantly feels triggered and wants to say all kinds of things back to Jack about how she's not just some chick and how Jack is the one who is letting alcohol ruin all his relationships, so who's really the weak one? Instead, he takes a deep breath, commits to ignoring his ego's demands to defend himself, and switches back into Emergency Empathy. He knows that he can address any valid points later when things are more calm.

MARK

Are you upset because you think I'm valuing
my fiancée's wishes over yours?

Jack answers in a slightly calmer tone.

JACK

Well, you pretty much are! And if I'm not there,
the whole family is gonna be gossiping about it endlessly.

Things still seem overly tense, so Mark decides to do another round of Emergency Empathy based on Jack's reply.

MARK

Are you concerned that your absence will damage your reputation
with our uncles and it might affect your friendship with them?

JACK

Yeah right. You know what? Do whatever you want. I don't even care.

Jack spoke the last line in a relatively calm tone, and even though Mark knows Jack doesn't mean what he's saying, he decides that Jack's tone is sufficiently calm enough to switch back into NVC.

MARK

(STEP 1)

Listen, man, the truth is, I would love for you
to be at my wedding. But based on what happened
at our sister's wedding when you got into a fight with

one of the groomsmen or at Dad's birthday
when you fell and hit your head on the table . . .

(STEP 2)

. . . I'm feeling really stressed . . .

(STEP 3)

. . . because I don't want something like that happening again,
which could ruin this day for us.

(STEP 4)

Am I making any sense to you?

Jack, looking dejected, nods in agreement.

JACK

I get it, bro. You're right. Do whatever you need to do. I'll be fine.

Jack's words indicate agreement, but the emotional connection between them still feels off. Mark doesn't want to leave it like this, so he decides to do another round of Emergency Empathy. Remember, Emergency Empathy can be used for a wide range of triggered emotions, not just for when someone is throwing insults and acting irate. A dejected or sad person can benefit from Emergency Empathy just as much.

MARK

Are you feeling upset because you want more support from me?

JACK

To be honest, I'm just embarrassed that
I'm forcing you to even have this conversation.

The connection level between them is growing but there are no potential solutions yet, so Mark decides to do one more round of NVC to see if it can lead to a possible win-win solution.

MARK

(STEP 1)

The whole family wants you to be there including Kate, . . .

(STEP 2)

. . . I'll be really sad if you're not there, . . .

(STEP 3)

. . . because you're my brother, I love you, and
I want to share this important moment in my life with you.

(STEP 4)

But if you come, you'll need to stay sober. I'm wondering—would you be open to the idea of going back to your AA meetings?

JACK

I don't know, man. I'll think about it. I gotta go.

MARK

Okay. No prob. Thanks for coming. I love you, man.
You coming to the pickup game tomorrow?

JACK

Of course.

MARK

Alright. See you there.

They hug each other and Jack leaves.

This was always going to be a very tough conversation, and though it may not be resolved, significant progress was created and that's what's important. Jack is now aware of the situation, and the choice to attend the wedding sober is ultimately up to him. Most importantly, the bond between the brothers is still intact, if not even stronger.

Mark was able to express his authentic concerns and honor himself and his fiancée while still honoring the love and bond he has with his brother. The conversation was authentic but never devolved into an argument because Mark applied many key strategies:

- He was able to ignore the urges of his ego to correct and defend against Jack's attacks. Not an easy task, especially with a family member who knows all your trigger points.
- He skillfully switched between Emergency Empathy and NVC at appropriate times.
- He never implied that his brother was wrong or bad at any time.
- He always sounded natural.

This is unlikely to be the only conversation they have on the topic because alcoholism is such a complex issue, but for the moment it's all that needs to be done.

It's important to remind yourself that not all NVC conversations have to end with a resolution, and it's okay if it takes more than one go at it. Some issues require more time to work themselves out, and this is perfectly reasonable. Some people might feel a sense of failure since there were no concrete solutions uncovered, but the reality is that this was a successful interaction because awareness of the problem grew as well as the connection between the participants. NVC and Emergency Empathy provide the tools to navigate these types of tricky conversations, allowing for deeper connection and growth even when the issues are tough or take time to work through. Whether the current solution works or not is irrelevant because they can revisit the issue and continue to work toward a permanent resolution. This is much different from having a heated discussion that ends with frustration and no solutions, leaving both parties reluctant to try again. In the next chapter, I will discuss a specific situation that commonly arises with these types of complex issues and explain exactly how to handle it. This moment can easily derail progress if not recognized, but with the right understanding and approach, it can become the turning point that leads to a win-win resolution.

9

The Threshold Moment

SOMETHING HAPPENED in my late teens that taught me a valuable lesson about Nonviolent Communication. It was a blisteringly hot summer day in Austin, Texas, and I was waiting for a metro bus that only came once every two hours. I had checked the schedule and arrived ten minutes early, just to be safe. The heat was relentless, and I couldn't wait to plunge into the ice-cold waters at Barton Springs, three miles away.

The bus stop was nothing more than a metal bench, fully exposed to the overhead sun on the side of a busy street near the university. After sweating there for fifteen minutes with no bus in sight, I felt a hint of annoyance: *Is anything on time anymore?* Knowing the bus never comes early, I was sure I hadn't missed it, so I ignored my discomfort and continued to wait. It was often five to ten minutes late. *No need to worry,* I told myself.

So I waited . . . and waited . . . and waited. When the bus was over thirty-five minutes late, and my shirt was sticking to my back, my mild annoyance had transformed into full-blown anger. Deciding I'd had enough, I put on my headphones, cranked up the music, and begrudgingly started the long, hot walk to the springs.

Not even one minute later, out of the corner of my eye, I saw the bus casually driving past me. I frantically tried to hail it down, but it kept rolling down the road without a pause.

I could barely comprehend what had just happened. After waiting over forty minutes in the scorching sun, how did I manage to leave at the exact worst possible moment? I couldn't have timed it worse if I had tried. To top it off, by putting on my headphones, I'd completely drowned out any chance of hearing the bus approach. It felt absurd, as if the universe was playing a cruel joke on me. Needless to say, it was a long, hot walk to the springs that day.

Fortunately I've since turned that aggravating experience into a life lesson that applies to NVC—a lesson I call the "Threshold Moment." A small but still significant percentage of Emergency Empathy attempts will work right away, often within the first or second try. These moments are wonderful when they occur, but in my experience, they're somewhat rare and not to be expected. More often, resolving conflicts requires a greater degree of effort and sometimes a considerable amount of skill, patience, and determination. These are the instances that typically contain a Threshold Moment, and they also tend to yield the most profound results. I discovered the Threshold Moment phenomenon after noticing it show up again and again, both in sessions with my clients and in my own NVC interactions. Once I became aware of it, I started seeing it occur in nearly every challenging exchange. I realized it was a true game changer, and I knew I had to share it with my students.

The Threshold Moment occurs after you've patiently and skillfully used NVC and Emergency Empathy for several rounds but feel like you're not making any real progress. You've diligently followed all the steps. You're not triggered, nor are you speaking in barely disguised tones of annoyance. You've switched between NVC and Emergency Empathy at the right moments, digging deeper with each round, yet somehow nothing seems to be working, and frustration is beginning to creep in. Just like with my bus, in NVC there is often a critical point where we feel tempted to give up. We feel frustrated because, despite our best attempts, nothing seems to be working and we're ready to just walk away. Yet if we can recognize this as a Threshold Moment and push through, we will often find that the breakthrough we were hoping for is just around the corner.

You may have been talking for what feels like an eternity, and though things haven't escalated, it seems as if you're getting nowhere. Every attempt to go deeper is met with one-word answers or vague, surface-level responses. No matter what you try, it feels like you've hit a plateau and the connection you're seeking remains out of reach. The thought crosses your mind: *I have no idea what else I can possibly do. I've tried everything! This is impossible. I give up.*

This is it! You've hit the Threshold Moment—the point when you feel like throwing in the towel, convinced that you've exhausted all your options. Walking away now seems like the only reasonable course of action and continuing might even make things worse. But here's the truth: This is a sign that you're actually close to a breakthrough. It's darkest before dawn, and if you can just hold on a little while longer, you can experience the glorious sunrise. Walking away now would be the exact wrong move at the exact wrong time if you want to succeed in NVC, both in the short and long term. If you can learn to recognize and embrace this uncomfortable feeling, your ability to resolve complex conflicts will skyrocket. It's not intuitive, but neither is Emergency Empathy. Yet they both work.

When you reach the Threshold Moment, the most important thing to do is stay the course. Do not give up. Recommit your resolve and do another round, making sure to follow the fundamental principles. If you're feeling particularly frustrated, take a deep breath and try a new approach. Acknowledge the frustration you're feeling and consider bringing it up. For example:

> We've been talking for over twenty minutes now, and I'm feeling frustrated because getting to a place of resolution for both of us is really important to me. But nothing I'm saying seems to be getting us any closer. Are you okay with continuing this talk until we both feel like we've reached a good place of understanding?

Statements like this will give you some time to breathe and reset. Trust that you are close. Stay calm and move forward. In my experience, after reaching the Threshold Moment, it often takes only one or two more rounds before the breakthrough happens. Guards drop and the true source of the conflict is revealed. Discovering the core reason causing the issue is often the biggest step toward finding a solution. Don't be like me as a teen, giving up on the bus just before it arrives. Keep going and you'll reach the promised land of conflict resolution and deeper connection again and again.

WHY DOES PUSHING THROUGH WORK?

Difficulty in finding a resolution to a conflict can occur for many reasons. However, if you're doing NVC correctly—using real feelings, not implying the other person is wrong or responsible for how you feel, and continually going deeper—then the lack of resolution is likely tied to a deeper issue. It often involves a lack of trust and connection or not feeling safe enough to open up yet.

For instance, imagine a parent trying to get their teenager to open up. The teen might want to tell them everything but knows if they're too honest, they may get punished. So they remain guarded. This dynamic isn't exclusive to parent-child relationships; it plays out in many situations where people don't feel fully safe to express their true feelings even though deep down they may want to. However, this lack of trust also has its own threshold. It can only withstand so many genuine attempts of Emergency Empathy before it gives way, opening up a pathway to honest and productive communication. When you reach the Threshold Moment, know that it might only take one more round of Emergency Empathy before the floodgates open and the person finally reveals everything they've been holding back. Often this release comes with tears, laughter, or some other form of emotional catharsis, leading to a deeper connection.

Sometimes the person you're talking to may not even fully understand why they feel upset. They may feel the emotions intensely but struggle to explain the underlying cause. You can continue making educated guesses with Emergency Empathy, but if they don't provide much feedback, it could be because they themselves don't know the real issue—until they hear it said aloud. Hearing something articulated can trigger an aha moment, resonating deeply and releasing pent-up emotions. Deep down, they may be craving appreciation, trust, or safety, even though their words may not reflect those needs. This is why it's important to keep going. If they're upset, there's always a reason and it can be discovered, though it may be buried underneath layers of confusion.

Here is an example to illustrate this point: Phillip and Marla have been married for nineteen years. They have two teenage children, and they are celebrating their anniversary with a weekend getaway. They've been excitedly planning the trip for months, but on the morning of their departure, Marla seems upset. Phillip waits for her to bring up what's bothering her, but she remains silent.

They have a four-hour drive to get to their cabin. After an hour of silent driving, Phillip decides to do some NVC to see if he can uncover the cause of her behavior.

PHILLIP

(STEP 1)

Hey, babe, we've been driving for an hour,
and you haven't said a single word.

(STEP 2)

I'm feeling concerned . . .

(STEP 3)

. . . because I really want us both to have a great time on this trip.

(STEP 4)

Is there anything on your mind that you'd like to talk about?

Perfect NVC, but Marla answers with an aggressive tone.

MARLA

I just want to be quiet, okay? Is that too much to ask?

Phillip feels hurt but avoids taking it personally. Instead, he decides to try Emergency Empathy.

PHILLIP

Are you feeling worried about how the kids will handle being alone this weekend?

MARLA

No, they'll be fine.

She doesn't give him much to work with, so he tries again with another round.

PHILLIP

Are you stressed about how much this trip is going to cost us?

MARLA

The whole world doesn't revolve around money.
Some things are more important than money, okay?

Phillip starts to feel frustrated. He's trying his best to remain calm and uncover the issue, but Marla isn't being very helpful. He takes a deep breath and reminds himself not to take it personally. He tries again, this time changing up the pattern.

PHILLIP

Does what's bothering you have anything to do
with something I said or did this morning?

MARLA

No.

Phillip is starting to feel like he is running out of ideas. He waits a moment to see if she says anything else that may give him a clue as to what's bothering her, but she stays silent. Phillip thinks to himself, *I am completely out of ideas! She's not giving me anything to work with*. He wants to give up but instead decides to do a round of NVC since she seems relatively calm.

PHILLIP

(STEP 1)

We have four days together, . . .

(STEP 2)

. . . and I'm starting to feel worried, . . .

(STEP 3)

. . . because I don't want whatever's bothering you to ruin this time we've carved out for each other.

(STEP 4)

Does that make sense to you?

Marla sits there in silence, refusing to reply. Phillip gives up. He's met his Threshold Moment. He thinks to himself, *I've tried everything! She's being impossible right now.* His ego tells him, *You should just turn around and go home if she's gonna act like this!*

Then he remembers the concept of the Threshold Moment. He realizes he needs to ignore his ego's wishes and stay the course. He takes a deep breath and decides to do another round of Emergency Empathy. He racks his brain to come up with another possible reason she might be upset. Nothing is coming. Everything seemed great until she got in the car to leave. He tries to put himself in her shoes and says to himself, *If I were acting like she is, why might I be doing that?*

Still nothing, but he knows he needs to say something or this will likely get worse. Phillip makes sure to speak in a calm and civil tone, despite his inner frustration and without much hope.

PHILLIP

Babe, are you upset about something that I have no idea about?

To his surprise, Marla starts crying and grabs his hand. He pulls over and holds her while she gets a good cry out.

MARLA

I'm sorry. I'm upset but I really shouldn't be, and it's not your fault.

PHILLIP

That's okay. Whatever it is, you can tell me.

MARLA

It's just that I thought I was pregnant, and even though I know that's not in our plans, I let myself get excited. But then I took two tests this morning and they both turned out negative, and I just feel so devastated.

Suddenly Marla's behavior makes perfect sense to Phillip. His frustration melts away, replaced by understanding and empathy. He's relieved that he remembered the Threshold Moment and gave it one more try—without it, their weekend might have taken a very different turn. This is the power of pushing through the Threshold Moment. It won't always be the very next round after you meet your threshold, but in my experience, it usually happens soon after. When you persevere, the breakthrough comes.

I would like to highlight one more item about this example. I've discovered that there is significant power in his last Emergency Empathy question: "Are you upset about something that I have no idea about?" This is a very effective phrase when used at the right time. I believe its power has to do with the inherent humbleness contained within it and the openness it allows in the response. It can work wonders, but only after enough connection and trust have been built. If Phillip had led with that question, it's unlikely it would have worked so well. But since he had already made several attempts to connect without blaming or judging, each round built more trust, even though Marla wasn't openly showing it. By the time he came to the final round of Emergency Empathy, the connection was strong enough for her to share her true feelings, and the breakthrough occurred.

I highly recommend keeping this phrase in your Emergency Empathy tool kit, but it's important to use it only when enough connection has been built. Trying to use it on the first or second Emergency Empathy attempt will drastically reduce its effectiveness. I would suggest only using it after a minimum of three rounds of Emergency Empathy as a general guideline.

10

Simplicity and Patience

KEEPING THINGS SIMPLE is one of the cornerstones of success in both Nonviolent Communication and Emergency Empathy. When communication is simple, it's easier to understand and keeps the conversation grounded and productive. A common mistake I see with my students is trying to cover too much at once. They'll often try to address three or four issues in a single statement, or pack way too much detail into one of the steps. Other times they will start off great and hit each step perfectly . . . then keep going and end up confusing everyone by overexplaining and repeating themselves.

This tendency to overcomplicate things is something I've noticed more often in my students who are already skilled communicators. By skilled I mean they're able to express themselves with accuracy and detail, they are cognizant of a wide level of emotions, they can see both sides of issues, and they are highly empathetic. All of these are valuable qualities and have undoubtedly served them well in many situations. However, when they attempt to do NVC or Emergency Empathy, there is a tendency to create information overload. They will make five or six valid points in one statement, but the person they are talking with only remembers one or two, and if they're triggered, you can guarantee it will be the ones that offended them the most.

Anytime you speak more than a few sentences at a time during a highly charged NVC interaction, it's going to be very hard for anyone, including yourself, to really grasp all the implications of what's being said. This will lead to layers of misunderstanding and frustration. The more you say, the easier it becomes for the other person to respond with vague statements that may sound like progress but really aren't, as it's unclear what they mean or what point they're commenting on.

For instance, let's say we have Devon and Alexis, a married couple who have been together for six years. Devon has always been a very skillful communicator, but if he makes four or five points about his feelings—his ideas about his wife Alexis's possible feelings, unresolved issues, possible solutions, and future concerns—Alexis could simply reply, "Okay, I see what you mean." But does she really? Does she understand and agree with every point he made or just a few? How will Devon know? Can either of them precisely repeat all the points he just brought up? Unlikely, especially if anyone is triggered. If Devon had only brought up one thing at a time, it would be clear what Alexis was responding to.

This is an essential understanding. Slow down and take your time. Not everything needs to get solved at once. Start with the most pressing issue or, depending on the situation, with the smallest. Either way, take it step by step. NVC works best when it is distilled down to its simplest form. Often you'll discover that solving one issue all the way down to its root cause will end up simultaneously solving multiple seemingly unrelated issues.

In another example, let's imagine Josephine and Dennis are engaged but have been encountering three major issues concerning jealousy, sharing finances, and physical connection. They both know these need resolution before they marry, so they sit down with the intention of using NVC to find solutions. In this example, both members of the conversation are aware that these tools are being used. Dennis begins by trying to address all three issues at once, which has him talking for a long time. Instead of a conversation, it feels like a lecture, leaving both feeling overwhelmed. Josephine suggests tackling one thing at a time, and they decide to start with her jealousy.

After several rounds of NVC and Emergency Empathy, they uncover that her jealousy is stemming from a miscommunication that occurred months ago. She had misheard something he said, which led her to believe he had been lying to her. Though it was over something insignificant, the fact that he would lie about anything had damaged her trust in him. Once this miscommunication is resolved, she feels relieved and closer to Dennis than she has in a long time.

They move on to discuss the finances issue. She feels hesitant about sharing a bank account with him, while he believes it's essential for a healthy marriage. Through their conversation she realizes that her reluctance is coming from a lingering lack of trust, rooted in the same miscommunication that had sparked her jealousy.

Now the connection between them is so high that it becomes obvious the third issue, a lack of physical intimacy, is also arising from the same source. What seemed like three separate issues turned out to stem from a single lack of trust. Once they restore trust, all three issues are resolved. This is a more common occurrence than many people may expect and is another reason why it's important to tackle issues one at a time.

LECTURE VERSUS CONVERSATION

I sometimes observe my students attempting NVC and speaking for several minutes without any response from the other person. No matter how eloquent or accurate you are, if you don't pause and get feedback along the way, you won't truly know what the other person is comprehending or if they agree or disagree with your perspectives. Without this understanding, the exchange can quickly shift from a conversation into a lecture, and it's very easy to tune out a lecture.

What we want is an engaging conversation that brings about mutual understanding. A helpful rule of thumb: Whenever you find yourself talking for what seems to *you* like a long time, take a moment to pause and ask the other person, "Is this making sense to you?" Listen closely to their response and adjust accordingly. When well done, NVC and Emergency Empathy will rarely require lengthy monologues. Instead, brief, thoughtful exchanges are more likely to keep both people engaged, aligned, and moving toward resolution.

SPECIFICITY

When in doubt, get more specific. This is an extremely effective principle to remember when applying Emergency Empathy, particularly in challenging moments. Since every situation is different and nuanced, there's no one-size-fits-all rule that will work every time. Instead, we have general rules and tips.

Often in the first rounds of Emergency Empathy, I'll begin with more general questions, gradually getting more specific based on their responses. Other times, it may be the opposite. However, I'm always aware that when I want results, the more specific I am, the more likely they are to occur. For example, I might start with a more general question, such as, "Are you feeling upset about something that happened at work today?" If the issue relates to work, their answer will likely reveal a clue I can use to craft a follow-up question with more detail. However, if they respond in a way that suggests work isn't the issue, I might get more specific about a different topic: "Are you feeling stressed about running into my ex tomorrow at the wedding?"

General questions are easy to brush off with a general answer that may reveal almost nothing, but specific questions, even when incorrect, tend to result in more specific responses, such as, "No, it's not that at all. I guess I'm just stressed about going on the cruise next month. I'm not sure we can afford it." This is a very powerful and effective concept to keep in mind. *Specificity leads to specificity, and generalities lead to generalities.*

Sometimes my questions progress in a linear fashion, growing more precise based on each reply. Other times, I switch topics altogether, especially if I'm truly in the dark about what might be bothering them. I might move from asking about work to politics to relationships, adjusting based on any small clues they provide.

Let's illustrate these ideas with an example. Lori comes home from work and finds her husband, Ryan, smoking a cigarette in the backyard and eating candy. She knows him well enough to understand that he only does these activities when something is seriously bothering him. She sits down beside him and gently starts with a general Emergency Empathy question.

LORI

Are you feeling upset about something that happened today, honey?

RYAN

No, I'm fine. It's nothing.

Lori knows it's more than "nothing," but since he hasn't given her any clear hints, she decides to try a more specific guess.

LORI

Are you feeling stressed about spending
the weekend with my parents next week?

It's just a shot in the dark, but since it's more specific, she's hoping for a more specific response.

RYAN

No, babe, I love your parents. I'm looking forward
to spending time with them. I'm just . . . I don't know.
I'm just being silly. I don't really want to talk about it.

Lori doesn't want to pressure him to open up if he's not ready, but the fact that he said "it's silly" probably means he does want to talk, but he's embarrassed. She decides to do a round of NVC.

LORI

(STEP 1)

We don't have to talk about it if you really don't want to.
It's just that, in the past, whenever I see you smoking out here,
it usually means something is really bothering you.

(STEP 2)

And one of the great joys of my life is to . . .

(STEP 3)

. . . be here for you whenever you need me.

(STEP 4)

So do you mind if I just sit out here with you for a while?

Lori just did very skilled NVC and it sounded very natural because she allowed herself to not rigidly follow the format, yet she still followed all the fundamental principles.

For **STEP 1**, the *observable fact*, she talked about her thoughts more than an observable occurrence, but it served the purpose of bringing attention to the issue, which is him being visibly upset, without implying he is bad or wrong.

In **STEP 2** she relayed that she is feeling joyful to have an opportunity to be there for him, without using the normal phrasing of *I feel . . .*

With **STEP 3**, she avoided the normal phrasing of *because it's important to me* or *I value* but still implied that she values being there for him.

Lastly, **STEP 4** was a connection-based request that was very gentle and allowed for him to easily accept her presence.

They sit there in silence for a moment or two, then Ryan offers up something that gives Lori her first real clue as to what is bothering him.

RYAN

We really need to get rid of that tree soon.

Ryan is referencing a tree that fell in their backyard after a recent ice storm. Lori replies in normal language without trying to do NVC or Emergency Empathy.

LORI

I thought you were going to buy a wood chipper today.

RYAN

I was, but the one I really want is too expensive,
and every time I think about buying a cheaper one,
I can hear my dad's voice telling me to never skimp on tools.

Ryan's father passed away three years ago. Lori goes back into Emergency Empathy with more specificity, based on what he has been revealing.

LORI

Are you feeling concerned that if you buy the one you really want,
it'll put us into a bad position financially?

RYAN

Yeah, I guess. I don't know why it's bothering me so much. It's not that big of a deal. I can just buy a used one.

Though Ryan agrees, Lori senses the tension hasn't lifted. Something still feels unresolved, so she tries another round of Emergency Empathy.

LORI

Are you feeling sad that you can't talk about this with your dad and get his input?

Tears immediately start streaming down Ryan's face.

RYAN

I just miss him so much.

Lori now understands that this was the real issue the whole time and is able to comfort him.

Ryan, like many people, can at times be disconnected from his feelings, especially such a deep one like grief. He didn't realize that what was really upsetting him was missing his father. He thought it was about the wood chipper, and thus he was embarrassed it was bothering him so much. The moment Lori brought up his father, it released a flood of emotion, and it was obvious to both of them that this was the real issue. She was able to do this because she never overcomplicated the conversation by attempting to address multiple topics at once and instead patiently brought up things one at a time. Everything sounded very natural and normal. She never got anywhere close to sounding like a lecture and was even comfortable sitting in silence with him. She also started off with simple general questions and gradually got more and more specific until the true reason he was upset was clear. This is the type of skillful communication that is possible when you begin to get comfortable and confident with these techniques.

11

Dealing with "Difficult" People

THE PAIN BODY, as we discussed in chapter 1, is the part of us that can transform someone who is normally sweet and loving into someone verbally aggressive or combative. For most people, this is simply part of being human and is a manageable and occasional experience. However, in group settings and communities, you will inevitably encounter individuals whose pain bodies at times dominate their behavior. These individuals can exhibit extreme and challenging traits: They may be chronically disagreeable, narcissistic, hostile, aggressive, or even abusive, sometimes to the point of enjoying the pain they cause others. While they represent a small fraction of society, their presence is a reality we must learn to navigate.

When dealing with these types of individuals, the principles in this book still apply, though these encounters are likely to be very challenging. Barring the threat of physical violence, I still recommend following all the steps as outlined in this book. However, if physical violence seems plausible, I recommend avoiding contact unless absolutely necessary.

The first thing to focus on when dealing with anyone who is triggered is to uncover the true source of their upset. They may be hurling insults or threats, and the intensity can quickly escalate, so it's very important you stay calm and avoid taking anything personally. Keep doing Emergency Empathy until you have identified the true source of the issue. Without this clarity, no genuine resolution is likely to be found, and if you start looking for solutions too soon, things may rapidly escalate for the worse.

It's important to remember that most people don't speak directly. They will rarely tell you what is truly going on with them and instead will speak in vague ways. You must read between the lines and take into account several factors, including body language, word choice, and especially the feeling in the room. Once these are all congruent, you can rest assured you are getting closer to the truth.

WHAT IF THEY MAKE NO SENSE?

Sometimes you may encounter someone whose behavior seems utterly incomprehensible, even irrational. You try Emergency Empathy, but nothing resonates because you can hardly fathom how a rational person would respond in the way they are. In these situations, it's essential to give them the benefit of the doubt. Assume that even if their reaction seems wildly disproportionate or illogical to you so far, there must be a rational reason behind it; something that, if discovered, could make everything make sense. Focus on uncovering this and ignore any thoughts that suggest it doesn't exist. This is you acting in good faith. When you believe there's a logical basis to their behavior, it becomes easier to find out and understand what's behind it. In contrast, if you assume their behavior is simply irrational, you're likely to get stuck making half-hearted guesses, which will likely end in frustration for both parties.

For example: Imagine working as a cashier at a grocery store and you accidentally short a customer ten cents. No big deal to most people, but imagine if the customer all of a sudden started crying, accusing you of purposely trying to rip them off and creating a huge scene. The instinct might be to think they're a little disturbed or emotionally unstable, but this wouldn't help if you genuinely want to de-escalate the situation. If you instead assume there's more to their reaction and do some Emergency Empathy, you might discover that they recently lost a loved one and uncovered significant hidden debts left behind by that person. Under this enormous emotional strain, even a minor perceived slight, such as being shorted on change, could feel like another betrayal or injustice.

By approaching the situation with empathy first and a willingness to understand, you create space for genuine connection. When we assume the worst, it leaves little room for a productive interaction. Many times, with patience and good faith, seemingly incomprehensible behavior will suddenly make sense, and you'll be able to respond in a way that helps rather than further escalates the situation.

Let's use an example to illustrate these ideas. Franklin owns a duplex that he rents out to two families. One day he gets a call from one of the families and learns that Jason, the renter next door, is acting irrationally and creating a scene in the front yard. Franklin is disheartened but not surprised to hear this. He and Jason served together in the military and are old friends, but this isn't the first time he has had behavioral issues.

When Franklin arrives, he sees Jason walking in circles in the front yard, angrily talking to himself. He also notices that the front door to Jason's duplex is damaged, possibly from being kicked, and there is broken glass on the porch. He sees the neighbors looking from the window, holding a phone ready to call the police. Franklin assesses the situation and feels no threat of violence, so he approaches Jason. He starts the conversation normally, instead of jumping right in with Emergency Empathy.

FRANKLIN

Jason, what's going on? Are you okay?

JASON

You too? I knew you were in on it, man!

FRANKLIN

Where is Evelyn? Is she okay?

Evelyn is Jason's wife, who is nowhere to be found. Jason completely ignores Franklin and continues walking in circles and muttering to himself angrily. Franklin realizes Jason is too agitated to have a normal conversation. He decides to try Emergency Empathy now to see if he can break through and uncover what is truly bothering him.

FRANKLIN

Are you upset because you and Evelyn got into an argument?

JASON

Wasn't no argument! How can we argue if she's over
at his house? Don't be stupid, man.

Despite the insult, this response was actually a sign of progress because it was the first time he directly engaged with Franklin's words. This demonstrates the power of Emergency Empathy. It can cut through even when someone is in an extremely agitated state and nothing else is working. Ignoring the insult, Franklin persists with another round of Emergency Empathy.

FRANKLIN

Are you angry because Evelyn has left you for someone else?

JASON

No, man, she's at her dad's with the kids.
She freaked out because she thinks I'm drinking again.

Franklin, feeling like he's homing in on the core issue, delivers another round of Emergency Empathy, this time varying the pattern.

FRANKLIN

So what's going on right now is that she thinks you've been drinking, but you really haven't been?

JASON

It was just one drink, man!

With each response, Jason grows a little calmer, progressively moving from extremely upset to upset, to slightly upset, and beyond. He suddenly stops walking and sits on the ground and leans against a tree.

JASON

It was supposed to only be one drink, but it got out of hand. I really messed up this time. I may have lost her, man.

Tears start streaming down Jason's face. Though Jason is clearly sad and remorseful, Franklin can see that the anger and extreme agitation in him have calmed down sufficiently enough so that they can now start looking for solutions and next steps.

FRANKLIN

(STEP 1)

I want to let you know that I'm gonna sit out here
with you as long as you want me to, . . .

(STEP 2)

. . . and I'm really happy that I'm getting a chance
to show up for you . . .

(STEP 3)

. . . because our friendship is important to me
and you've always been there for me when I needed it.

(STEP 4)

Let me know if you want to go inside and grab some coffee
and a bite to eat. Otherwise I'm gonna take a seat right
next to you and we can just hang out here.

This is not likely to be an easy fix and will probably take many conversations and possibly professional help to manage. The important thing to keep in mind, though, is that with just a few rounds of Emergency Empathy, Jason is out of his highly agitated manic state, no one was hurt, and the bond between Franklin and Jason remains strong, if not stronger than ever.

The conversation started with Jason basically ignoring Franklin and getting more and more worked up with every passing moment. There were many strategies that Franklin could have tried that would most likely have only made things worse. He could have:

- Tried to speak calmly and use logic.
- Warned him that if he doesn't calm down, the neighbors will call the police.

- Threatened him with eviction.
- Berated him and pointed out how he is making everything worse with his behavior.

However, because of Jason's high state of agitation, each one of these strategies had a dismal chance of helping even in the slightest and most likely would have made things considerably worse. This is because when someone is in a triggered state:

- Calm logic will almost always be completely ignored or interpreted as some form of attack.
- Any mention of the police could easily increase their fear and agitation level.
- Any threats of eviction will likely be seen as an attack.
- Any language implying they are bad and wrong in any way will likely put them on the defensive.

Emergency Empathy is one of the only possible peaceful resolution strategies available in situations like these. No matter the agitation level, stick to the fundamental principles and you can have great success from the smallest to the most intense conflicts. Even one well-timed Emergency Empathy attempt can turn a potentially dangerous situation into a healing interaction.

12

Advanced Techniques

THERE ARE MANY STAGES you may pass through on your NVC journey. I went from an overconfident beginner to an underconfident beginner in record time. My first real-life attempt at NVC worked so well that I thought I had it all figured out. Then my second attempt was a complete disaster. Though my intentions were good, I unquestionably made the situation worse. This is normal. There will be a learning curve, and sometimes the best teacher is failure. Failure is deeply humbling and embarrassing but if you let it, it can become great motivation to study more and truly integrate these principles. Be gentle with yourself when you fall short and acknowledge the courage it takes to try something new.

With patience and diligence you *will* improve. Remember, you are rewiring communication patterns that have been operating for most of your life. Regularly return to this book and the other sources you have found helpful. This will keep your skills sharp and give you a strong chance of staying on the right track.

As you progress from beginner to intermediate and beyond, you will likely discover certain phrases or approaches that work particularly well for you. This is a good sign, and I encourage you to experiment as long as you stay within the core principles. In this chapter I will show you some helpful concepts and tools that I have found especially useful in my journey.

SELF-EMPATHY

Emotions can sometimes have an air of mystery to them. You might wake up one day feeling sad without any clear reason, or you might find yourself irritated without being able to pinpoint a specific cause. You may even feel a wave of depression creeping in, despite everything in your life going smoothly on the surface. In these moments, doing rounds of Emergency Empathy on yourself can be surprisingly helpful. Start guessing and see what resonates. You can do it aloud, in your head, or write it out. Choose whichever one you prefer.

Despite its simplicity, it's a powerful process and works very similarly to doing it with someone else. You'll know you're getting somewhere when the intensity of your negative feelings begins to ease. If you still feel the same after a few rounds, continue digging deeper. Try seemingly unrelated topics until something starts to resonate. Once you're able to identify what's going on within you and why, it will take the edge off of the negative emotions that are occurring. You can then operate from a place of clarity and understanding as you work toward a solution.

There are also times when either you or someone else might feel triggered, but it may not be appropriate to speak up and use Emergency Empathy right then—for instance, if you're in a work meeting and get upset after hearing an executive implying things about you or your team that are untrue while they're giving a presentation onstage. This is probably not a great time to interrupt them with Emergency Empathy and disrupt the meeting.

In these situations, self-empathy can be invaluable. Instead of sitting there and silently fuming at the injustice with no outlet for these feelings, try doing a few rounds on yourself. Become a neutral detective whose job is to identify exactly how you're feeling and why. If you're able to pinpoint the source of your discomfort, the feelings often become less overwhelming, and you'll likely find yourself feeling more centered and in control. This way you will have a greater chance of staying professional and can address the issues at a more appropriate time.

SILENT EMPATHY

This whole book is about speaking with others to build connection and de-escalate conflicts, but doing Emergency Empathy on someone else doesn't always need to be aloud. Imagine sitting on a bus and noticing someone several seats away visibly triggered and causing a disturbance. If you feel yourself becoming irritated or judgmental, try doing a few silent rounds of Emergency Empathy on them, guessing how they might feel and why until something resonates. Though you have no way of knowing whether your guesses are accurate, the process can still help. Even if you never have an interaction with them, there will still be a benefit to you because your feelings toward them will soften and thus your internal state will improve. This shift in perspective can also influence your demeanor and body language in a positive way in case you do interact with them.

In fact, whenever you catch yourself silently judging someone from a distance, switching to silent Emergency Empathy can be immensely beneficial. Judgmental thoughts usually carry a feeling of negativity and disconnection, reinforcing a sense of separation—one of my least favorite states. Emergency Empathy, on the other hand, builds a sense of understanding and connection, even if it's entirely internal.

PREPARATION

If you're anticipating a difficult conversation, preparing in advance can be very helpful. Start by writing out your opening NVC statement, ensuring it aligns with the fundamental principles (no judgment, no blame, real feelings). Make sure it feels authentic to you and brings attention to the core issues you have been experiencing. Try crafting a few variations, as this will help you see the situation from different angles. Next, imagine the person taking everything you say negatively and becoming triggered. Then come up with as many Emergency Empathy responses you can think of. I recommend aiming for at least five or ten, each with a different feeling and value. This will make you dig deep and uncover some of the less obvious possibilities.

These responses are not meant to be memorized and spoken word for word during the actual interaction. Even if you're a skilled actor, reciting memorized lines will most of the time come off as phony or inauthentic. Instead, this exercise is intended to familiarize yourself with potential responses so that you're not trying to think of them for the first time in the heat of the moment, especially while you're under attack. The more prepared you are, the easier it will be to remain calm, dodge the attacks, and execute proper NVC and Emergency Empathy. Writing out multiple responses will also likely soften your stance and make you more empathetic toward the other person as you will naturally understand their perspective more. This will naturally come across in your demeanor and gives the whole interaction a much better chance of being productive.

If necessary, you can bring notes to remind you of ideas, but otherwise stay present, speak with authenticity, and trust that your preparation will pay off.

WHEN SOMEONE USES NVC AGAINST YOU

When practicing NVC and Emergency Empathy with someone close to you, especially a partner, it's common to encounter some resistance from time to time. Occasionally people may feel like NVC sounds formulaic or even manipulative, leading to reactions such as frustration, sarcasm, or refusing to interact. They may suspect that you're trying to "fix" them rather than having an authentic conversation. This can be especially true when you're still learning and sometimes make fundamental mistakes.

If you sense your partner's frustration building, I recommend immediately switching into Emergency Empathy. For instance, if your partner rolls their eyes or makes a sarcastic comment when you try to use NVC, an Emergency Empathy response might sound like:

- "Are you feeling upset because you think I'm trying to control the conversation?"
- "Are you feeling annoyed because you don't think I'm being present and authentic with you?"
- "Is the main issue you're having with me doing NVC that you don't have confidence in me doing it correctly?"
- "Are you feeling frustrated because you think NVC is manipulative?"
- "Are you feeling concerned because you suspect I'm trying to fix you instead of accepting you as you are?"
- "Does the core reason you would prefer me not to do NVC have to do with past experiences you have had with it?"

Make sure it sounds as natural as possible. Feel free to bend the rules in these moments in favor of sounding natural, except for the fundamental ones, such as being nonjudgmental and never implying they're bad or wrong. Once you have accurately identified what the source of their discomfort is, you can switch into an NVC statement to express why it's important to you to use NVC and Emergency Empathy.

(STEP 1—OBSERVATION)

Thank you for sharing that, and I understand
where you're coming from.

(STEP 2—FEELING)

I feel concerned about giving up on NVC . . .

(STEP 3—VALUES)

. . . because this relationship is important to me
and I want to do everything in my power to ensure
we're able to resolve our conflicts while strengthening
our connection instead of building resentment.

(STEP 4—REQUEST)

Would you be willing to try it out for a few weeks
and then we can revisit it again to see if it's helping?

It's worth noting that learning and applying NVC can initially be uncomfortable for everyone involved. Both you and your partner are likely to experience moments of tension, misunderstanding, or even impatience as you work to build new patterns of communication. Changing lifelong habits is almost never going to be easy. True growth rarely is. Acknowledging these moments as part of the process and an opportunity to grow together, rather than a sign that NVC isn't working, will lessen the discouragement.

OTHER HELPFUL TOOLS AND TECHNIQUES

Aside from NVC and Emergency Empathy, I would like to share a few additional tools I've discovered on my journey to becoming a better communicator. Though not a part of what I learned from Marshall Rosenberg, each can be used alongside NVC and Emergency Empathy and can significantly deepen your ability to navigate complex interactions.

Steel Man Argument

The *steel man argument* is a technique that can help avoid hours of needless argumentative debating. It's essentially the opposite of a *straw man argument.*

A straw man argument is when someone misrepresents or oversimplifies another person's position in order to make it easier to attack or refute. Instead of engaging in good faith with the facts, they attempt to make the other person's position look silly and unreasonable by leaving out key information or distorting details. This usually results in an unproductive and frustrating argument, instead of an edifying debate.

A steel man argument does the opposite. This is when someone does their best to present the strongest, most robust version of the opposing view, even improving upon the original argument if possible, before attacking or refuting the position. This approach shifts the goal from "winning" to understanding and uncovering the best ideas. Instead of creating animosity or defensiveness, it builds mutual respect and encourages collaboration in the pursuit of truth. The person who hears their perspective strengthened and fairly represented is less likely to take a combative stance and more likely to remain open to hearing the opposing view.

When we have an attitude of win at all costs, the frequent cost will be peace within the relationship. Pursuing truth over being "right," on the other hand, will serve to strengthen the relationship. The person you are talking with will feel heard and understood—similar to reactions as a result of practicing Emergency Empathy—so there will be no need to repeat, talk over each other, or use ad hominem attacks. The next time someone presents an idea that you think is flawed, before you disagree with them, to the best of your abilities improve on their idea and verbalize it. If they approve of your take and agree that it's an accurate representation, now you can present your opposing idea and explain why you think it's better than even the best version of their idea. This often encourages the other person to do the same for your position, leading to a constructive dialogue where the best position will become clear sooner rather than later.

I have used this countless times, and it almost never fails to create a spirited but enjoyable dialogue that quickly gets to a place of resolution.

Working with Anger Issues

There was a time when I was passionate about learning how to day-trade stocks. Every morning I would wake up and trade the opening of the market, and almost every morning I would lose. It was infuriating. I was studying all the time, taking tutorials, listening to mentors, and still I kept losing day after day. Every time I would lose, I would get angry. The more I lost, the angrier I would get, and over time it became more and more intense. I would get so angry some mornings that my anger would poison the rest of my day. There would be times I would yell so much at my computer screen that I would blow out my voice. I am a musician in my spare time, so this was a big problem. The final straw was when, after a particularly frustrating morning of losing, I kicked my kitchen garbage container and it flew against the wall and almost went through a window. That incident was a wake-up call: I needed to find a way to manage my anger immediately.

At first I tried to suppress my anger by ignoring it. I focused on not expressing outward anger at all, no matter what I was feeling inside. This tactic helped give my mornings the appearance of calm, and my trading did improve a little bit. The problem with this strategy, though, was my anger didn't disappear. It shifted. I found myself drawn to watching violent videos on the internet, which was uncharacteristic for me. I realized this was my suppressed anger looking for an outlet.

I knew I needed to find a different solution because ignoring it was clearly unsustainable and taking me to dark places. I went to the internet and started searching for answers. My initial goal was to learn how to control my anger, but I quickly realized the real goal should be how to not let my anger control me. Eventually I found an effective, surprisingly simple technique from an unexpected source, a YouTube channel titled *The Crappy Childhood Fairy*, run by Anna Runkle. She's built a career around teaching this method, which she originally learned from an Uber driver. It's very simple, anyone can do it, and it genuinely works. Within days, my anger issues improved drastically. What would usually escalate me to an eight out of ten in anger now only took me to a three. This was a vast improvement and exactly what I was looking for. I was able to continue my day-trading journey without any window casualties or ruining my days with a lingering foul mood.

She offers the technique free on her website, podcast, and YouTube channel, but I will summarize it here for you, though I highly recommend checking out her offerings as well.

This practice involves a brief, twice-daily writing exercise. The first part is to write down all of your fears, whether big or small, logical or illogical, petty or profound. It doesn't matter if they seem silly or minor. As long as they're connected to your personal fears, just put them down. No need to worry about sounding brilliant or proper punctuation unless you would prefer to. Mine often looked like this:

> I am afraid of losing, I am afraid of wasting my time, I am afraid of never getting good at this, I am afraid of making dumb mistakes, I am afraid of losing my job, I am afraid of doing something dumb, I am afraid of being greedy, I am afraid of being left out, I am afraid of being homeless, I am afraid of nuclear war, I am afraid of sleepwalking, etc.

Some fears I would think are silly. Some I wouldn't even be

sure I meant, but I would write them down anyway, stream-of-consciousness style. Once I couldn't think of any more fears, I'd delete everything. This isn't meant for anyone else to read, not even for my future self. The aim is to bring these fears into the light, because once they're acknowledged, they lose much of their hold. Hidden fears are far more damaging than acknowledged ones.

The next part is similar, except you write out all the people you resent. It doesn't have to be proper NVC or even deep resentment. This is again more about getting out every idea that comes to your head, knowing this will be deleted as soon as you're done. It's important to phrase it as follows: "I resent (*name*) because I'm afraid (*reason*)." Here's what that could look like:

- I resent John because I'm afraid he will not show up to work tomorrow.
- I resent Jenna because I'm afraid she is lying to me.
- I resent Danny because I'm afraid he doesn't like me.
- I resent Nina because I'm afraid she won't stop drinking.

Write out every resentment you have—new or old, strong or weak, imagined or real—and then delete it.

Now it's time for a quick meditation. A five-minute meditation will suffice, but if you want to go longer, that's fine too. I usually just sit in a comfortable position and focus on my breathing while I let go of any thoughts that try to grab my attention. I also find it helpful to listen to the silence around me. If I focus on the silence, it almost becomes like a soft roar and somehow that relaxes me and helps me keep my focus.

That's it. That's the nuts and bolts of the practice. I highly recommend it for anyone struggling with anger issues. My anger issues are a thing of the past ever since I added this into my daily practice.

PRACTICE GROUPS

Once you feel comfortable with all the concepts in this book, the next step is to practice. However, especially in the beginning, I recommend you practice with supervision. You certainly don't want to practice bad habits, and without a skilled supervisor, that is what is almost guaranteed to happen. Find an online or in-person group run by someone you trust and give it a few months. There's a lot of nuance to getting Emergency Empathy and NVC correct, and it will take a decent amount of repetition before you'll be able to pull it off on a consistent basis in the real world. If you stick with it long enough, though, the results will be profound, transforming every one of your relationships and enriching your communication for life.

CONCLUSION

Learning to communicate more effectively is a lifelong journey, one that will consistently bear fruit as long as you continue to apply the principles. Yet it's important to keep in mind that if you stop practicing, all of these habits can fly right out the window, rarely to be heard from again. Doing NVC and Emergency Empathy is not like riding a bike; you can very easily forget how to do it properly if enough time passes. This is one of the reasons I started writing books and making podcasts on the topic. I want to regularly be reminded of NVC. It's easy to be lured into complacency, especially when you are not actively having conflicts in your life. This lack of practice is more likely to arise in people who are single or spend a lot of time alone, but rest assured that as soon as a significant relationship develops, conflicts will develop right alongside. This is natural and normal, so you will want to keep your conflict resolution skills sharp.

Even if your life happens to be temporarily conflict-free, I still recommend refreshing your memory at least once a month on the fundamental principles and techniques of NVC. You can reread a chapter of a book, listen to a podcast, analyze an argument from a film, or mentally replay a recent moment of irritation and imagine approaching it with NVC instead. Anything that helps you actively engage these tools will strengthen them. This strength is absolutely crucial, or you will likely find yourself out of practice when the inevitable intense conflict makes an unexpected appearance.

The benefits from these skills are not limited to close personal relationships—even though that is where they truly shine—but are also valuable in professional settings. For example, you cannot slander someone if you are speaking in facts, which is an important skill for newscasters, public speakers, politicians, podcasters, and writers, to name a few. Knowing how to quickly de-escalate triggered people is enormously useful for teachers, police officers, coaches, parents, therapists, and negotiators. Many a business deal gone wrong could have been saved if one of the parties applied Emergency Empathy when things got intense. The truth is that the wisdom in these principles can positively affect nearly every aspect of one's life and work. I truly believe that there is no one in the world whose life wouldn't be improved by learning NVC and Emergency Empathy.

Remember, this is an art and not a rigidly predefined formula. Human interaction is far too nuanced for strict rules to be effective in every situation. You will make mistakes, but don't dwell on them. Notice them, correct them, and keep moving forward. Focus on the core principles of nonjudgement and authenticity. These will take you far and keep you close to the true essence of nonviolent communication.

As you leave these pages, I encourage you to keep a playful and open attitude as you experiment with these principles. Know that truly every conflict is an opportunity for deeper connection. Every intense interaction is a chance to choose authenticity over pretense, curiosity over accusation, and empathy over judgment. If you ever feel lost or discouraged after a frustrating interaction, don't forget to give yourself credit for at least attempting to improve the quality of your relationships with these new skills. Then return to the principles, revisit these tools, and begin again. There is no shame in missteps; the only true failure is giving up, and the willingness to keep practicing and learning imperfectly, courageously, and consistently is what will ultimately guide you to becoming a great communicator.

RESOURCES

Without a doubt, my number one recommendation for further study is Marshall Rosenberg's original book on NVC, *Nonviolent Communication: A Language of Life* (PuddleDancer Press, 2015). Available in audio, e-book, and paperback, it is, in my opinion, the most effective, clear, and powerful resource on the subject. Nearly everything you need to understand and practice NVC is contained within its pages.

Rosenberg also left behind a rich library of additional books and recorded seminar teachings, many of which are available for free on YouTube. I highly recommend exploring those as well, but only after you've grounded yourself in the original work.

I recommend my first book, *The Art of Nonviolent Communication: Turning Conflict into Connection* (pub. by author, 2019), in audio, e-book, and paperback, available on Amazon. I also recommend my podcast, *The Art of NVC*, which is freely available on most podcast sites. Both the book and my podcast can also be accessed through my website, ArtofNVC.com.

For those who wish to deepen their practice more quickly, I highly recommend finding a guided practice group. These are great places to explore these principles in real time.

Marshall Rosenberg's books and recorded seminars were my primary sources of learning. I have not personally explored many other NVC programs, so I do not offer specific recommendations beyond his work, but that doesn't mean there aren't other great resources out there. I encourage you to explore and see what resonates with you as long as they are in alignment with the fundamental principles.